CHAIM KLEIN was born  :l.
His life has been cotermi :e.
He is married to the jour ée
Solomon, and lives mainly in London, ns
and two grandsons. English is his third working language.

GROWING UP WITH ISRAEL

a memoir by

Chaim Klein

ISBN 0-936315-49-0
STARHAVEN, 42 Frognal, London NW3 6AG
books@starhaven.org.uk
https://starhavenpress.wordpress.com/
https://www.facebook.com/starhaven.org.uk/

Typeset in Palatino Linotype

in memory of my parents

with mother outside of our home in Samorin

A Note on the Text:

There are some fifty sections to this book, each marked by a significant topic or event in that period of my life. The reader may skip and choose as he wishes, but I have decided to run the narrative continuously. I beg the pardon of those who might prefer a formal demarcation of contents.

ANCESTRY AND BACKGROUND

I was born on the 12th of January 1947 in the Jewish hospital in Bratislava, today the capital of Slovakia but at the time of my birth part of Czechoslovakia. I was told that the families of both my father and mother, who lived in small towns near Bratislava, had lived in their respective homes for over 200 years. This is supported by the family plot in the old Jewish cemetery (established in 1736) of the spa town Piestany, where my maternal great grandparents and grandmother's grandfather are buried. There are other tombstones with my maternal grandmother's surname, Urban, one of which seems to have both Urban and Abarbanel, but I don't know if or how the people buried are connected to my family. I was told by Tibi, a cousin of my mother, that the Urban family originated from Spain, from which they, with all the Jews, were expelled in 1492. They moved to Holland and over many years levitated eastward, until settling in Piestany. The tombstone with Abarbanel and Urban written on it, indicating a possible change of name from Spanish to a common local name with similar sounds, may confirm this tale told from father to son. In Surany, my father's town, most of the Jewish cemetery has been destroyed and vandalized and I could not find any of my ancestors' tombstones; all that is left are photos.

On 26 June 1946 my father obtained an official copy of his birth certificate, perhaps in anticipation of emigrating. From it I know the birth years of my grandparents. My paternal grandfather, Heinrich (Chaim in Hebrew) was born in 1871; his wife, Ida (Adel in Yiddish) née Fleischer, in 1879 and my father, Jozef (Yosef in Hebrew), on 28 September 1904. Heinrich died in 1932 and his wife in 1933; my father told me that his mother died from heart break. Similarly, from an official copy of my mother's birth certificate dated 28 July 1937, I know the years of birth of my other grandparents: my maternal grandfather, Frantisek (Pinchas in Hebrew) Schmiedel, was born in 1880, his wife, Regina (Rachel in Hebrew, I think) née Urban, in 1886 and my mother, Anna (Chana in Hebrew) on 6 January 1914. I can work out from the tombstones in Piestany, one side in Hebrew, the other in German, that my mother's maternal grandmother, Theresa (née Kohn), was born in 1862 and died in 1924; and my mother's grandfather, Sigmund, was born in 1857 and died in 1930. I have a copy of his death certificate, his death announcement and permission to transfer his body from Vienna, where he died, to Piestany. I can't read the dates on the tombstone of Reuven Urban, Sigmund's father and my grandmother's grandfather, but Mordechai Shmuel Urban, who I believe, but am not sure, was Reuven's father, died in 1875. He would be the grandfather of my great-grandfather. My mother told me that Theresa's father, my other grandmother's grandfather, Kohn, was a rabbi in one of the towns near Piestany. My father was the second of eight siblings and my mother the last of four. My father's family were traders, buying local agricultural produce, processing feathers for example, and selling locally and beyond. They also brought in coal and other products for sale locally. My father spoke little of the past but some years ago a suitcase with letters, all in German, between the two sisters-in-law of my father's sister was found. One lived in the then Palestine, the other in Czechoslovakia. One of the letters from Czechoslovakia describes the engagement of their brother to my father's sister. The future sister-in-law complains that their brother did not ask what dowry his fiancée would bring; she adds that on second thought, given the wealth evident in the house, the number of eminent rabbis present and lavishness of praise they heaped on the family, the brother did not really need to ask. My mother's father, who was not local (I do not know where he came from) dealt in textiles, did well, went into a partnership which did not succeed, lost his money, and moved from Bratislava to Samorin, where he opened a textile shop. My mother was taken out of school to help in the shop as she knew how to sew; her two sisters were married by then and the brother lived and worked in Vienna. It was always clear that my mother adored her elder brother, Philip. Louis, a younger cousin of my mother's living in Paris after escaping Communist Czechoslovakia in 1968, told me that Phillip worked for a large company in a senior position. Phillip and he used to play violins in cafés and restaurants in the evenings in Vienna.

The ill-conceived Munich agreement in September 1938 transferred the Sudetenland from Czechoslovakia to Germany. On 6 October 1938 Slovakia used the political chaos in Europe to declare autonomy. On 14 March 1939 Slovakia moved even further and declared independence under German protection; the next day Germany annexed and invaded the Czech state. Slovakia was ruled by a pro-Nazi party headed by Father Jozef Tiso. Already in 1938 Jews were targeted by the authorities, which introduced anti-Jewish measures including confiscation of property and businesses, firing Jewish government employees and forced labour. A census in 1940 stated that there were 89,000 Jews in Slovakia, about 3.4% of the population. In addition, there were about 45,000 Jews in the area transferred, with Nazi Germany's support, from Slovakia to Hungary in 1938. Both Surany and Samorin were in the territory transferred to Hungary, while Piestany, and of course the capital Bratislava, remained in Slovakia. As a result, some of my father's and my mother's families were in Slovakia while some were in Hungary. Reading about the fate of Jews in the two countries leaves an impression that there was a competition between them as to which would be more brutal. Hungary also had a pro-Nazi government. My mother, who had no difficulty speaking about her ordeals, was deported to Auschwitz together with her parents. They were taken by cattle and freight trains; from photos one can see that it was a struggle for people to climb onto and get out of the carriages, as there were no steps. I recently checked some details of these horrible journeys: there were 70-100 people in each carriage; the journey lasted two to four days; there was little food and water and one bucket for a toilet in front of everyone, which was very smelly and often got full. Adults held the children as there was no room to sit; people started to die, and their bodies were used as seats. On arrival came 'selection'; one direction led to immediate death in the gas chambers, the other to work and therefore life for now. My mother was directed one way and her parents the other as they were considered too old to be useful workers. My mother did not know what it was all about and wanted to go with her parents to continue helping them, so she ignored the instructions. Someone, she was fairly certain it was the infamous Dr Mengele known as 'angel of death', lifted and pushed her to the other side, the side of life. That was the last time she saw her parents. I do not know how her siblings died but Tibi, told me that he believes my uncle died at the end of the war on one of the death marches.

My father was married before the war but I do not know if he had one or two daughters. I was always under the impression that he had one, but I was told a few years ago by one of my father's cousins a few months before she died, aged ninety-six, that he had two. My father was a slave labourer and eventually sent to the concentration camp at Mauthausen in Austria. The camp started around a granite quarry and continuously expanded. I began to read about conditions in the camp, but they were so bad that I was unable to carry on. Zvia, my only cousin, told me recently that her mother told her that my father worked in the gas chambers at Mauthausen. Mauthausen's principal method of killing inmates was by extreme hard labour, very little food and no medical treatment; the average life expectancy was just a few months. The gas chambers and crematorium were used to kill but mostly to dispose of bodies of those who had died for other reasons. My father's wife and daughter, or daughters, must have been sent to Auschwitz; the wife would have been selected to die as the Nazis thought that grieving young mothers would not be good enough workers. One of my father's brothers was with him in Mauthausen; both were ill with typhus, the brother died. The possibility that my father had to handle his brother's body in the crematorium haunts me. Mauthausen was one of the last camps to be liberated, after which my father returned to Surany. One sister and her husband survived as they had escaped to Hungary with false papers, but their daughter, who was left with another sister as they thought she would be safer that way, was killed. One can imagine how the parents felt until their dying days. As it happened, my father's first wedding was together with the only sister who survived; the double wedding was split technically over two days, one just before sunset the other just after, not to mix the two celebrations. I do not know how the other siblings of my father died. When my father's sister, who returned to Bratislava, heard that one brother had returned, she arranged for a horse and cart to bring him to her, a journey of about 40 kilometres. My father recovered with the help of this sister.

My mother also returned to her home in Samorin, but no one else of her immediate family came back. My mother, just before deportation, had buried in the garden some items which she now recovered; in addition, she went to the neighbours' homes and identified items that had been taken from her home and recovered those too. Among these items were embroideries for Shabbat and for Passover that she had made as part of her Bat Mitzva tasks; my aunt said the maid must have helped my mother. I use the Shabbat one every Friday night; I also use the other one in Pesach for the three matzot on seder night. Also recovered were one hundred beautiful hand-painted china pieces. My mother told me they were a wedding gift to her parents from an admirer of her mother's who was heart-broken when he was rejected. According to my mother, he was especially upset when he saw who was preferred to him; the admirer owned the china factory. I have about thirty of the china pieces and some other items my mother recovered. Only one thing was recovered from my father's home, a damaged Megilat Ester or Scroll of Esther on klaf or parchment.

My parents were very different from each other. My father was strictly observant and had studied in a yeshiva, or religious seminary; as far as I can judge, his secular studies were limited to mathematics as he was very good at it but did not know much about literature or other subjects. His first wife was the daughter of the local shochet, or ritual slaughterer, and they were childhood sweethearts. My mother came from an assimilated background; while her father was observant, her mother's large family of 13 siblings, was not. They loved music in all forms, were artistic and generally sophisticated, cultured and talented. My mother and her eldest sister were friendly with two sisters who were my father's cousins, so the families knew of each other but no more than that. When it became clear that my father's wife had not survived, his sister set about finding a wife for him and introduced him to my mother. It was common to introduce survivors through a common connection; it was practical, but also people wanted to hold on to something familiar from the past. My mother told me that in the course of their first meeting, my father informed her that he would always love his first wife. My mother's reaction was that that was fair enough, but one had to try to carry on as best as possible given the tragedies everyone had suffered. My mother thought, given how successful my father's family were in business, that at least financially they would be secure. She did not know that my father, unlike his brothers, was not commercially minded; he was too straight.

My father had to obtain permission to marry from the Beit Din of Bratislava, as the death of his wife was quite certain but there was no absolute proof. This permission, or ctav haiter agunot in Hebrew, gives details of the first wife (her first name was same as my mother's) and states that my father would agree to abide by the ruling of the Beit Din should his first wife reappear. It is kept in my safe for my descendants, together with a certificate issued to my mother on 21 August 1945 by 'Trustee of the Slovak Council for Social Solicitude', listing the camps she had gone through: Osviecim (Auschwitz), Krakow and Feldafing. The certificate (no S 24394) is in three languages: Slovak, Russian and English. It says, 'Call at the reparation authorities with this certificate! Keep it at all times to assist your safe return home!' (English is used in the certificate.) I also have my parents' Ketubah, or marriage certificate.

My parents got married in February 1946; there is only one photo of the wedding and it looks bleak. They must have moved between Samorin, Surany and Bratislava. I don't know what my father did; his social security booklet from 1947 and '48 is stamped by his brother-in-law's stationary business and my mother's cousin's textile business. I also don't know what kind of life we had, but in photos I look a happy child playing with toys and in the snow. There are photos of me with my beautiful cousin, Zvia, who was born six months before me and lived in Bratislava. Looking back at my early years with my parents, I can see that my mother had chosen what I call 'life', trying to leave the Holocaust behind, while my father was not able to do so fully. Many survivors continued to live the Holocaust in one way or another. The most obvious were writers, Primo Levi, who took his own life, and K. Zetink who, while giving evidence at the Eichmann trial, fainted and seemed unable to adjust. My father never said a word about the Holocaust and seemed unable to be happy; he kind of went through the motions of life as a necessity, without enthusiasm. I felt the sufferings of both of my parents, but there was a difference; my mother would sing and be happy, but my father was always serious and silent. Only later did he start to smile and tell jokes.

EMIGRATING TO ISRAEL

On February 25, 1948 Czechoslovakia, until then the last democracy in postwar Eastern Europe, became communist. Since the role of the Slovak government in the Holocaust is a contentious issue even today, it is not surprising that the new regime banned discussion of it. Once it was possible, my parents, like most Jews who survived in Czechoslovakia, left for Israel and never, not even for a visit returned. They were restricted on what they could take; my mother managed to sell her house for a small sum but could not take it out of the country, so my parents bought stationery and other such items in the hope of turning them into cash in Israel, at which they did not succeed. My father did not manage to sell his house and just left it. Our journey with my aunt Cornel, uncle Jeno and their daughter Zvia, in May 1949, was on lorries to a transit camp near Trieste, where we waited for three weeks, then travelled by boat to Haifa. The port in Trieste is known as Shaar Zion, or the gate to Zion, as so many Jews used it to go to Israel, both before and after WW2. I hope my parents had a chance to visit the beautiful large synagogue and other sites in the city; if they did, they never mentioned it to me. The boat we travelled on was called *Galilah* and was very old, built in the US in 1913. I was told that conditions on it were terrible and my father and his sister were unwell the whole journey. I had a dummy which apparently fell into the sea and my parents could not get me a replacement, which was how I was cured from using a dummy. Zvia remembers herself, me and her father standing on deck as the ship approached Haifa and her father pointing out Mount Carmel. I have my father's teudat oleh, or new emigrant certificate, No 23111. I don't know how the numbering of these certificates worked but there must have been, since the establishment of Israel, hundreds of thousands of immigrants before us. Most of the new ones from war-torn central and eastern Europe or from Arab countries were refugees with few possessions and little or no knowledge of Hebrew. We arrived on 6 June 1949. *Galilah* was scrapped in 1953. I'm not, of course, comparing our exodus to the exodus of my forefathers from Egypt. The

Biblical Exodus had Divine involvement, while in the years leading to our exodus, I don't know where the Divine presence was. But our exodus was tortuous enough, and I think my descendants should know my story, in addition of course to the Biblical one.

My father was able to read Hebrew but could not speak it, and my mother knew no Hebrew. I can imagine the chaos and confusion with thousands of immigrants arriving in the small, one-year old country. My place of birth was recorded incorrectly, and I discovered the error and my correct place of birth only in 1991; similarly I discovered the local Slovak name my parents gave me at birth only in 2015, long after both parents had died. My parents and I got consecutive ID numbers. We were sent to a maabara, or transit camp, called Shaar Haaliya, or the Gate of Immigration, just west of Haifa; there we lived in a tent. On 12 July 1949 we were moved to Gelil, today Glilot, just south of Herzlia to, as I was told, a slightly improved 'home', built from corrugated metal. I found a photo of the Gelil maabara and it had tents, so we may have started in a tent there also and were only later 'upgraded'. A few years ago, I read that conditions in these transit camps were very difficult; with hundreds of people per toilet and water tap, they were dirty and smelly. Around the same time, Israeli television had two programmes about the maabarot, and the horrible discomfort came across vividly; all newcomers were disinfected with DDT – only later was it discovered that DDT is cancerous. The programmes revealed that police had to guard the maabara to prevent people escaping, and the perimeter was surrounded with barbed wire. In one of the programmes a policeman who had been a guard in such a camp described seeing hungry children, skin and bone only, resorting to theft. There was even rebelliousness against the maabarot managers. I don't know what my parents and other Holocaust survivors thought of being again in a camp surrounded by barbed wire. It must have been very hot, with flies, mosquitoes and other unpleasant creatures. I was told that the first new word I learned in Israel was mouse, but I don't know in what language it was, as my parents spoke Slovak, Hungarian, Yiddish and German. German was their mother tongue and my father told me that in youth, if his parents heard any of their children speak anything other than German, they were spanked!

Conditions were so bad that I became ill and was unable to swallow food. There is a stamped note in my father's teudat oleh that we were entitled to three months medical care; either my parents did not know how to get it, or it was not accessible, or such help as was offered was inadequate. My condition got worse and my mother, in desperation, took me to Tel Aviv to my uncle's sister, the one I mentioned who'd come to Israel in the thirties and was corresponding with the other sister who remained in Czechoslovakia. I don't know how my mother made the trip, how she found the right place, 4 Yona Hanavi (the prophet Jonah) Street near Allenby Street close to the sea, but she got me there and I was left there for a few weeks and brought back to life. Rachel, the daughter of my uncle's sister, was then twelve or thirteen, and she remembers me lying motionless. Today the building in 4 Yona Hanavi, like many of the buildings around it, is a hotel.

On the 2 August my father released from customs two wooden crates valued at 210 Lirot ($600) and another crate on 10 August valued at 70 Lirot ($200) containing the belongings we had been allowed to take out of Czechoslovakia; I have the document relating to this. On 1 December we moved again, to a transit station within Gelil. I believe that other families known to my parents from Surany, Samorin and other towns in Slovakia were in the same maabara, which must have helped. My uncle had a small amount of money and he found, in Haifa, a small flat not completed yet; he paid demei mafteach, or key money, making him part-owner/part-tenant. I have many memories from this flat; one room was the living-room during the day and at night we rolled up the carpets and opened up the sofa into a double bed where my aunt and uncle slept. The other room was a dining room-cum-study and my cousin's bedroom. Both my father and uncle started working as night guards at the Israel Electric Corporation. My uncle remained until retirement, progressing from night guard to chief accountant of the Corporation in Haifa. I remember as children, during summer holidays, Zvia and I had to be very quiet as my uncle slept during the day. In later years Israel introduced help packages to assist new immigrants, quite different from these early days of the state.

1950, original houses & building the road

CREATING THE MOSHAV

My parents and many new arrivals ended up creating new moshavim or cooperative agricultural settlements. A moshav is a community of families guaranteeing each other so that no one will go bankrupt. It is less sharing than a kibbutz; for example, each family's finances are separate and private. Over the years the moshav, like the kibbutz, evolved and changed, and in the early years no one had any money or assets so the arevut hadadit, or mutual guarantee, did not have much of a financial meaning; but it was powerful as social and moral support. The moshav was managed by an elected committee which received no fee; a few salaried employees ran the administration, finances and communal purchasing and marketing of what was produced. Each household purchased from the moshav food, seeds, fertilizers, water, the use of equipment etc. All the produce of individual members was delivered to a centre point, weighed and marketed collectively. Purchases and sales were recorded and at the end of each month the cost of purchases was deducted from the income from sales, and some people accumulated large negative balances. The centralised buying and selling brought obvious benefits and savings. The first moshav was established in 1921; within a few years of the establishment of the state of Israel the number of moshavim exceeded 400. This was to help find work and accommodation for the new immigrants, many of whom were unskilled. It also helped to ensure food for the whole country. Anyone who wanted to join a moshav had to be approved by existing members; a candidate usually lived in the moshav for a trial period before voting took place. At some stage, to help with finance, many of the moshavim, ours included, introduced paper money useable in the moshav only; this lasted for some years. The notes were a simple affair, made of relatively thick paper with black printing on one side only. Today, collectors, including me, look for them; I don't have any from my moshav, but I have some from other moshavim and kibbutzim, which I buy whenever I find them.

When I was young, I took it for granted that we lived in the moshav and that was it. I was not envious of people living in towns. In fact, because of the Zena, or rationing, in the early years of Israel (up to 1959) we were better off as we had enough food. But once I went to the army, and after, I sometimes wondered if living in the moshav had been the right choice. Existence was difficult; we never had money, and we lived in appalling conditions. I can see that for my father it was, under the circumstances, kind of all right: we had open space, no one was his boss, we were near the synagogue, the community generally was religious and he made friends. For my mother on the other hand it was most unsuitable; culturally, and for some time also literally, we were in a desert and she was not made for the hard physical, agricultural work. Nevertheless, she was not bitter, and she made friends too, though occasionally she made unflattering comments about the place and some of its people. Work on the farm was particularly difficult as no one could afford to buy equipment, so primitive methods were used. My mother told me that she had wanted to join a different moshav, called Batzra, in the centre of Israel near the towns of Raanana and Kfar Sabba – she had some friends who went there – but my father wanted to go to a moshav in the south of Israel to be named Shafir, a place mentioned in the Bible by the prophet Michah (chapter 1; verse 11). Over the years, we would have been financially better off in Batzra as the value of the land is higher than in Shafir, Batzra being in a better location; it is also possible that my father would have been able to find a job in a nearby town. But my father did not want to go to Batzra as it was not going to be religious enough. Some of my mother's friends from there would visit us in the sixties and seventies, especially Karolla.

The idea of creating moshavim for new immigrants was brilliant. I doubt if the authorities foresaw all the positive implications; they probably had little time and few options. Houses and communal buildings, unsurprisingly of low quality, were built by the incomers, giving them work. The moshavim aided the security of Israel as they were built near borders and places of strategic importance. For Sepharadim, or Jews from Arab countries, the moshavim helped keep family life alive, unlike in towns and especially in what are known as ayarot pituach, or developing towns, where the old structures collapsed with nothing to replace them, resulting in long term problems. For many Ashkenazim, or Jews from Europe, the moshav replaced to some extent family members lost in the Holocaust. In our family for example, from over 100 uncles, aunts, grandparents, great uncles, great aunts and first cousins, we were reduced to seven: my parents, my uncle, aunt and three great uncles. My father had helped Arnold, his uncle, to escape Czechoslovakia at the start of WW2; Arnold first went to South America and afterwards New York, from where he visited Israel often. My mother's older uncle Julius, whom she had not seen since before WW2, lived in Paris, where I visited him in 1969 on my way to London; he died later aged 96. My mother's favourite and youngest uncle, Alexander, returned after liberation to the family home in Piestany, where he died aged 83 in 1984; my mother did not see him since moving to Israel, and I never met him. His ashes were buried in his father's grave in the family plot in Piestany.

My parents, with some other 100 families, were co-founders of the moshav. The first of the group arrived on 9 September 1949, but I don't know when my father got there. By an interesting coincidence, my mother and I moved to Shafir on 12 January 1950, my third birthday; I know this from what is written in the teudat oleh. The moshav was created in the fields of the Arab village of Sawafir, off the road connecting Gedera and Ashkelon, in the south of Israel. I think it was assumed that the Arab name came from the original Biblical name: Shafir, in Aramaic, means nice and proper. The land on which it and some of the neighbouring moshavim and kibbutzim were built is flat, fifty-eight meters above sea level. My first memories are from the time around establishment of the moshav, and what I recall most is mud and no roads. This is ironical because most of the time we suffered from heat, not rain. The summer months were so hot that at times it was difficult to breathe and too unpleasant to be outside in the middle of the day; on top of this there were flies, mosquitoes and ants everywhere. The moshav was built like T, two rows of houses, a row on each side of a long road, at the end of which were more houses 90 degrees to the left and right. At the centre, the houses stood away from the road to make space for communal buildings and facilities. Our house was number 17, the first house out of seven on each side in the centre; our side was called the Slovak neighbourhood as all seven families were from Slovakia. Each house had the land behind it, about fifty meters wide, all the way to the boundary of the moshav, which totalled about 28,000 square meters. It was not much. There is a story about an American farmer who visited Israel in the 1960s; he was taken to a moshav by an Israeli farmer, who proudly told him, 'Do you see the tree about half a mile away? All the land up to it is mine'. The American replied:

'What? It takes me half a day to reach the end of my land'. The Israeli replied, 'Ah, I had such a tractor ten years ago.' Our plot was a little different from others as it was not totally flat but halfway started to slope downwards. Along one side of each plot was a water pipe, on the other a dirt road. The pipe and the road were shared with the neighbours, which resulted either in great friendship or disagreement, quarrels or even total breakdown in relations. I should point out that the founders' disagreements did not carry on to the children: we had our own quarrels. While the dirt road was used by both families at any time, the water pipe was used by each family on alternate days. Over the years, a few families moved within the moshav, some to improved houses or locations that became vacant, others to get away from neighbours they did not get on with.

Communal buildings included the Beit Kneset or synagogue, zorchania or shop, machlava or dairy, mazkirut or office, mikveh or ritual bath, gan or kindergarten, machsan or store for agricultural equipment, moadon or place to play, have meetings and celebrations, mirpaah or GP surgery. A last building was a small secure place where guns were stored for guarding the moshav and possible emergencies. Initially buildings were built mainly from wood, corrugated metal and asbestos; only gradually were they upgraded. The moadon was left as it was, but a newer one, also from wood, was built next to it. The original synagogue was replaced by a proper but unattractive building; a more attractive synagogue was built in the late '50s with a donation from Sir I. Wolfson. I recall Wolfson's visit, accompanied by Moshe Moshkovitz, the energetic head of Moatza Ezorit Shafir or council for moshavim and kibbutzim in the region. While this synagogue was being built, it was used by us children as a place to play; Yosi Noi threw a stone from the upper floor, which hit my head; there was lots of blood and I can still feel the scar – in those days I had hair. The old synagogue was then adapted for other purposes; on its southern wall a big square patch painted white became a screen on which movies were occasionally shown. We would sit on crates and haystacks in the open air to see old American cowboy films. I recall being bewildered when I saw my first one: I could not understand how cows managed to walk on a building wall. Moshe Moshkovitz deserves special mention as he was instrumental in the creation and development of the whole area and active until his recent death aged 96. The emblem of the council of moshavim in the Shafir area is of a tree cut down with just the lower part of its trunk remaining, a green shoot coming out. This is as per the prophet Isaiah (11;1): 'There shall come forth a shoot... and a branch out of its root will bear fruit'. I very much identify with this: our parents were the roots, my generation the trunk, the third generation the branches and all following generations the flowers and fruit.

My parents, like most in Shafir, had no previous experience in agriculture; my father's profession according to his teudat oleh was socher or merchant. Also, my parents were among the older residents and not in the best health. As mentioned, we did not do well and had no money. Each household received, I think from the Jewish Agency, one cow and beds made of metal. The beds were more suitable for cows, but they were for us and we had them for years; they were called mitot Sochnut or Jewish Agency beds. Mules were also given but each mule was shared by a few families. The product of a horse and a donkey, mules are strong, stubborn and stupid. Over the years some families managed to acquire horses, and the number of families sharing each poor mule dwindled so that, in the end, by default, we became the sole owners of one. We had this animal for over two decades, but I was never attached to him. We treated him well, never hitting him; if we wanted him to go faster, we just rattled the reins on his back. By contrast, I was attached to the first cow we had. It was big and strong and, despite the fact that her horns had been cut off before we received her, she ruled over the other cows; she had character and was the cleverest and sometimes even helpful to us by trying, though not always succeeding, to keep the small herd disciplined. Each year our number of calves and cows increased slowly and at the height we had twelve cows and a few calves, all of them direct descendants of the original cow. I'm not sure but I believe that my parents and other members of the moshav had to repay the Jewish Agency for all they received.

We grew vegetables, mainly tomatoes, cucumbers and peppers, so we had plenty of food, but our inexperience coupled with the very hot sun resulted in most of our produce and that of other families being below a required standard and thrown into the rubbish. I helped my parents pick vegetables and put them into argazim, or wooden crates, and I remember that most of them had black spots from the burning sun. We took the argazim to a warehouse in the centre of the moshav, only to be rejected; to this day mountains of rotten vegetables are embedded in my memory. We also had some fruit trees: apple, plum, guava, quince, pomegranate and perhaps others, but they were only for our consumption as there were not enough of them. Each time a cow escaped the enclosure, it ran straight to the trees and would damage them. In any event we did not do well with trees either; I remember other families having big, beautiful fruit while we usually had not so nice fruit, and I had to go to old Mr Brown to buy big, beautiful plums.

MY MOTHER'S ILLNESS

My mother was in and out of hospital most of the early years in Shafir; she had problems with her eyes, totally blind in one and only partial sight in the other. On top of this, she had gynaecological issues as she was pregnant more than once but lost the babies. I remember her last pregnancy well as it was showing and some of my friends were teasing and saying that I was going to have a sibling. Most unfortunately, it did not happen. I would have loved to have had a sibling; all my life I was, and still am, hoping that my half-sister(s) would somehow appear. I always was a little jealous of anyone who had siblings.

While my mother was in hospital, I stayed most of the time at the house of my friend Rafi; at times, I even slept there. Rafi's family was also from Czechoslovakia, the same town as my paternal grandmother, but the majority in Shafir were from Hungary. Rafi's family lived five houses away; they and four families living near them continued to speak Slovak at home, but the vast majority, including my family, spoke Hungarian. Here we were in Israel but in practice the 'official' language in our moshav was Hungarian! Anyone who joined the moshav or worked in it had to speak Hungarian and, if they did not know it, they learned. The most striking example was two Arabs from Gaza who, after the 1967 war, came every day to work at the Tzeizler family farm; they learned Hungarian. I think it was Ephraim Kishon who wrote that Israel is the only country where mothers learnt their mother tongue from their children. In Shafir all the children picked up Hungarian and it was left to the grandchildren to teach their grandparents Hebrew. Years later my wife, Emma, and I visited Hungary and Emma commented, and I agreed, that most of the women in Shafir dressed and looked like the women in rural Hungary. Shafir was a diaspora island in Israel.

When I stayed at home, my father would make eggs for me; he was a better cook than my mother. At some stage Tibi's mother, my mother's aunt by marriage, lived at our home and helped. I also stayed, during my mother's illnesses, at my aunt and uncle's small flat at 43 Ben Yehuda Street in Haifa. I don't know how I got to Haifa as it was a four-hour journey by three buses. On at least one occasion it was winter, and I slept on the terrace as Baruch, Zvia's cousin from her father's side, who was studying engineering at the nearby Technion, also lived and studied there. The building was big with many flats and fronted onto the main road to Mount Carmel, which curved at the point where it stood. The road behind the building used to be called UN Boulevard, but after the UN equated Zionism with racism (on 10 November 1975) its name was changed to Zionist Boulevard. On that street, the house number was 63. My aunt's flat was on the third floor on Ben Yehuda Street but minus one floor on UN Boulevard. The building was a little way up the slope to Mount Carmel, and some cars did not realise that they were approaching a curve at the bottom and plunged into the buildings. Every day I used to go up UN Boulevard to the makolet or corner shop to buy fresh black kimel or herb bread. Just further up Zionist Boulevard is the well-known, beautiful landmark of the Bahai temple and gardens. The plus side of me being away from home was that I did not go to school. I used to accompany my aunt on her shopping trips to the shuk, or market, called Talpiut on bus number 4. She would position me in the centre of the market to guard the shopping and would bring me whatever she purchased so she did not need to carry everything all the time. I would then help to carry the shopping to the bus and the house. My aunt was efficient in everything she did. Zvia is the same. There were a number of families in the building who spoke Hungarian to me. Zvia had friends there and nearby and we played with them, both in the flats and outside around the building. Zvia had a particular whistling tune that I had to learn so that we could communicate without shouting if one of us was out and the other at home.

Once I stayed in Jerusalem with my mother's favourite cousin Tibi and his less favourite (in my mother's eye) wife, Aranka. The journey to and from Jerusalem was on a narrow, winding, steep road and I was petrified that the bus was going to fall into the ravine. At the time, Tibi lived in Kiryat Moshe neighbourhood in a lower ground floor flat; the windows inside were near the ceiling and outside at ground level and I was afraid at night. In the moshav, our shutters were made of metal for protection from Arab infiltrators called fedayeen who blew up homes, stole cows, equipment and caused whatever damage they could. But the flat in Jerusalem had no shutters on the windows and it was not easy to feel secure. I must have been about six or seven and, as we were taught religious law, I was shocked to see cars driving on Shabbat. We did not see many cars driving through our moshav and certainly none on Shabbat except an occasional military vehicle. Every day I went by bus from Tibi's home to see my mother who was in the Hadassah hospital in Ein Kerem in west Jerusalem. In my mother's ward was a pretty teenage girl who always played with me, and she was my first love.

Whoever came into contact with Tibi loved him. He was born 19 February 1915 and his Hebrew name was Ariel Shmuel. My elder son was born on 18 February and his name is Ariel Shmuel. Tibi was cultured, good looking, picked up languages quickly and had many friends. Because of work, he and Aranka later moved from Jerusalem, first to a cheap unpleasant area in south Tel Aviv, afterwards to Ramat Gan. In later years my mother visited them from time to time. Aranka would leave her with Tibi to chat and listen to music. During the war Tibi had suffered badly with his health and could not have children.

As my mother was nearly blind and had to put drops in her eyes a few times a day, I used to help her to manage simple tasks; one that sticks in my mind was putting thread through needles. But there was another thing I did not help her with; it was salt, which I never liked but both my parents liked and oversalted everything. My mother, because of her near blindness, often sprinkled the salt outside the dish, and I did not tell her. Over the years she got better at routine tasks and was able to put thread through a needle by feeling the needle. She was always petrified that she would become totally blind. Many years later she needed a cataract operation on the one eye she was able to see a little with, and she was scared. Eventually she agreed to have the operation and we paid for it privately in the Shaare Zedek hospital in Jerusalem. Because she was unable to see in the other eye and the eye she had the operation on was bandaged, she was blind for about twenty-four hours. I was with her all the time except the night, as there were other women in her room. In the bed next to her was a charedi or very orthodox woman who had many visitors, and I had to ask repeatedly for quiet. At some point the woman apologised to me and said that she herself was desperate to rest. Her husband was totally useless, and I arranged for a nurse to shut the door so that no one could come in. Generally speaking, Israelis are very helpful, and the visitors meant well but the effect was opposite to what was intended. Another woman in the ward was Arab and her very dedicated daughters had a rota so that one would be with her all the time. At night, the daughters helped my mother to the toilet. After she left hospital, I arranged for my mother to be in a beit havraah or convalescent home for a week in Motza near Jerusalem. Talking about help... Driving in Israel, as everyone knows, is dangerous, and many drive as if they want to kill the other road users; but if there is a problem or accident, those with murder in their eyes turn extremely helpful. One of Israel's best known writers, Amos Oz, wrote: 'I love Israel even when I cannot stand it. Should I be fated to collapse in the street one day, I want to collapse in a street in Israel'. Another general observation: people are friendly on public transport; total strangers talk freely with each other on the buses, and it is not uncommon to hear personal questions, particularly how much one earns. I used to be embarrassed by my mother's conversations at bus stops and on the buses. I never travelled with my father; he was too busy working.

EARLY YEARS

My father served in the Israeli army from 1 October 1950 until 15 April 1953 according to his certificate of discharge. His military number was 508317 (mine was 964816), and his duty was guarding. Ironically, around the age of fourteen I replaced my father unofficially on guard duty in the moshav. There was one paid person from a nearby moshav, Zrachia, who was on duty every night; with him, on a rota base, was a member of the moshav. Each member's turn was once every two or three months, depending on the number of members at the time. My father was so tired by evening that he was unable to stay up, so I filled in for him. I knew how to use a gun and looked older than my age; this was important, as often the army came to check if guards were patrolling the moshav. The permanent guard had facilities at the mazkirut (office), and with him I would drink very strong tea with a lot of sugar and nana.

The number of families in Shafir began to go down soon after its establishment. Anyone who had a relative who could help moved to towns like Bnei Brak (very orthodox) or Ashkelon (the nearest) and some even abroad. Most of those moving to Bnei Brak worked in cleaning common parts of houses and/or in kitchens of yeshivot. The houses in the moshav, comprising one room and one half-room, were, as mentioned, of poor quality, without foundations, so we had cracks everywhere. When it rained, if you touched the inside walls, your hands became wet as the bricks were more sand than cement. The roof had tiles, but the ceiling was a kind of paper glued and pressed together, painted white, and not much use as insulation. The floor was large grey paving stones; they may have been level when put down, but I recall them as uneven. We had no electricity and my mother cooked on a primus, a small creation made of metal. At the bottom it had a round container for paraffin and three metal posts pointing upwards to hold a pan above the fire; in the middle was a wick to light. We also used paraffin for light; we had to clean the glass as smoke from the flame would blacken it, and the walls and ceiling. We also had a mekarer or icebox; every day or every other day, someone came to the moshav in a horse cart, selling blocks of ice. He shouted kerach, or ice, and broke off different sized blocks which we put into the ice box; at the back of it was a pipe over a bucket to collect water as the ice melted. The iceman continued to shout kerach, kerach even after starting to use a bell; years passed before he changed from a horse cart to a lorry. We and others in the moshav continued to use an ice box long after we were connected to electricity as we did not have enough money to buy a proper fridge. Bread and paraffin were sold in a similar way. At some stage, my father used wood from the crates in which we had brought items from Czechoslovakia to build a kind of kitchen on the north side of the house and a shower next to it. The toilet was a small wooden hut twenty or thirty meters from the house; when the hole underneath filled up, we'd move the hut to a new position over a new hole, which we dug. Everything was primitive. For example, pipes were on the ground, so in winter the water was freezing – we had no means of heating it – and in the summer very hot. After some time, some pipes were covered with earth; this improved things, but by then I was used to having cold showers in winter.

For animals, a few simple structures were built, one for cows, one for chickens and another built later for general use. All these structures had asbestos parts and the last was completely made of asbestos. Over the years we added and enlarged them, continuing to use asbestos; this was before it became known that asbestos was a cancer risk. We also planted flowers and some trees for shade.

As time went by, everyone improved their living conditions. My father built a veranda at the front of the house where we kept newly hatched chicks until they were able to join the older chickens. I remember that once, in winter, when I was ill with one of the usual children's illnesses and my mother was in hospital, I was alone in the house. I spent my time on the veranda where we had a simple paraffin heater there for the chicks. Somehow I knocked the heater; the straw on the floor for the chicks caught fire, killing some of them and causing other damage. After that my father built walls with windows and a door, put tiles on the floor and eventually incorporated the veranda as part of the house. I've already mentioned that shutters were made of metal, because of the fedayeen. After the war of independence in 1948 borders were insecure; Gaza, to the south, was under Egyptian control and the West Bank, to the east, was under control of Jordan. Fedayeen would come from both Gaza and the West Bank, and Shafir was on one of the routes between the two. The first half of the 1950s was characterised by many deadly attacks on Israeli civilians and retaliations by the Israeli army. In April '56 two houses close to the entrance of our moshav were bombed. In one lived the Rosenroch family: their son, Yaakov, who sat next to me in class, was badly wounded and spent months in hospital; once he recovered, the family moved to North America, where they had relatives. The other house belonged to the Biterman family: they had a toddler who was sleeping in a cot; luckily, the toughened paper ceiling fell on the cot and protected the boy from the rubble. If the building had had a normal ceiling, he would have died. I remember the evening; I don't know if I heard the explosion and did not know what it was or just did not hear it. But I remember people coming to tell us to lock up and have no lights on; we still did not have electricity and were using paraffin. Next morning when we were on our way to school, we saw the damage to the houses: parts of the back and side walls collapsed. To this day I have a very clear picture of what I saw so many years ago. There were instances of stealing and damage to properties by fedayeen, but I don't remember any detail. In 1988 Shafir suffered another terrorist attack near the spot of this 1956 incident.

GROWING UP

Until the age of about seven I was often ill with a fever, and I was not very strong; it was recommended that my tonsils should be taken out. My mother did not like the idea and managed to track down a friend from Czechoslovakia who'd also come to Israel and who was an ear, nose and throat specialist; she checked me and did not think I needed the operation. She was right, as a few months later, I rebelled and did not allow my mother to decide what I should wear. My mother was overprotective (Holocaust survivors' syndrome), putting on me too many layers, and I remember being uncomfortable when I was running around playing with friends, sweating. I started to wear sandals and shorts even in winter and I did not have a coat at all and was never again ill. I don't know if the following is connected to my tonsils, but I had difficulty swallowing mushrooms that my aunt used to cook; my parents never had mushrooms. Until the time I rebelled, Zvia was much stronger than I was, but now she was in for a surprise. The relationship between Zvia's family and mine was close despite the distance and discomfort of the journey between Shafir and Haifa. Every Pesach and Succot they came to us for a week. I used to go to them for a few weeks in summer holidays. They knew nearly everyone in Shafir and everyone knew them. As the distance from the bus stop to our home was over a kilometre, I used to go and wait for them with the mule and a cart. Sometimes I waited for over an hour as it was impossible to predict when the bus would arrive. I absolutely admired my aunt, uncle and Zvia. Once I stopped being ill, even though I'd kept my tonsils, I started to help my parents. They did not ask, but I saw their struggle and, like most of my friends, wanted to help. The work made me strong and in one of my summer trips to Haifa I was suddenly stronger than Zvia, and it took her time to adjust. Zvia was my first boss and my being stronger made little difference to that. My aunt tried to protect me but without success. Usually Zvia and her mother conversed in Hungarian while Zvia and I conversed in Hebrew. Zvia would often call me, saying in Hebrew 'bo rega' meaning come for a minute. My aunt would complain in Hungarian: 'mar megint bo regasig' meaning she is doing 'bo rega' again. My aunt did not know what 'bo rega' meant but she knew that it was something to do with Zvia bossing me. Zvia and her parents conversed also in German and Slovak, so Zvia is fluent in about six languages.

In one instance of our playing/fighting, I knocked Zvia to the tiled floor of their terrace. For a few minutes her parents and I did not realise what had happened: I'd accidently broke one of her front teeth. For years, she suffered. I have apologised many times and here, once again, I do so. During those summer holidays we often went to one of Haifa's beaches: Bat Galim or Daughter of the Waves, which was a favourite of the British during the mandate years (1917-1948); Hachof Hashaket or the Quiet Beach; or the private beach of the Israel Electric Corporation, which must have been very polluted. Zvia took swimming lessons; I did not have money, so I watched what she was taught, and this was how I learnt to swim. Zvia's parents paid for me to enter the beaches. They sometimes also bought me clothes.

I'm sure it was great for Zvia to visit us in the moshav. For someone living in town, the open spaces, animals and clean air were a welcome change. Zvia liked to attend to the flowers and tidy around the house, which we sometimes neglected due to pressure of work. In one of her cleaning binges, she disturbed a poisonous snake of the zefa type. The snake got into the house; it was afternoon, and one of my mother's friends, Alice, was chatting to my aunt and uncle. Suddenly Alice saw the snake climbing in the corner behind my aunt and uncle. She screamed and they instantly left the room and closed its door. I called my father, but he was milking, and you can't stop milking in the middle; so after he'd finished, he came with a pick and killed the snake in one hit. If I recall correctly, my aunt and uncle were not happy that my father gave priority to the cows, but they came first always: we were slaves to them. As children, we knew which snake was poisonous and which not; we left them alone usually as they ate mice. One could see a lump in a snake's body after it swallowed a mouse; as it digested, the lump became smaller and moved along its length. There are forty-two different types of snakes in Israel. Only nine types are poisonous; all are nowadays protected.

with Zvia, my special cousin from earliest age

LIVING CONDITIONS

Once, in the 1950s, my father's uncle Arnold from New York came to visit. My mother, with the help of her friend Alice, tried to make the house as presentable as possible and prepared a nice meal, but Arnold was so appalled by our living conditions, so different from the grand homes my parents' families had had in Czechoslovakia, that he decided to send us a parcel every few months. He never came to visit again but stayed with his nieces in Haifa and Tel Aviv. The parcels would include items that Arnold no longer needed or wanted – shirts, trousers, shoes, jackets etc. My mother would immediately set about altering them, as my father was shorter than his uncle. Some she would alter so I was able to wear them, but they looked funny on me, especially the trousers. Arnold included ties, but what do you do with a tie in a moshav? My parents found a solution. Like most people in Shafir, every Thursday I would take a chicken or goose or duck or turkey or even pigeon to the shochet or ritual slaughterer. The animals did not like the ordeal and tried to run away, so my parents tied their legs with the ties Arnold sent from New York. This had a side effect on me: years later when Emma and I lived in London, I had to put on a tie for work; I had no idea how to do it, so Emma did it for me but all the time I saw in my mind the animals being taken to be slaughtered, and all day I felt as if I were destined for the same fate. You will understand why the minute I finished work, I took the tie off. It was some weeks before I could tie the tie by myself, and I cursed in Arabic during the process. We were good at cursing in both Hungarian, as we heard from the adults in Shafir, and Arabic, which we picked up from everywhere else. Cursing in Hebrew was not so common; perhaps it is because for so long Hebrew was not a living language but used only for praying and studying holy texts. A side note: in those days we were not aware of animal welfare and the chickens were kept all the time in cages, with artificial light in the evening so they would continue to lay eggs. We also used to feed turkeys, geese and ducks by opening their mouths and dropping in corn. We did not think about this, but it is forbidden nowadays in Israel, as it is forced feeding.

Our number of cows increased, so we stopped growing vegetables and concentrated on them. My father got up around five a.m. to do the feeding and milking; we also made cheese and butter. After delivering milk to the machlava, he would go straight to the synagogue for shacharit, or morning service. During slichot or the period for penitential prayers (before Rosh Hashanah and Yom Kippur), all the men in Shafir got up around four a.m. and milked the cows after slichot. As children, we usually said slichot at school just before morning prayers, but I went with my father a few times to say slichot. The scene of everyone draped in the tallit, or prayer shawl, praying for forgiveness left a lasting impression on me. As for the daily routine... the cows were again milked every evening, and during the first weeks after giving birth they were milked also at lunch time. Milking was by hand: one would sit next to a cow on a low-level chair with a bucket, wash the four nipples and do two nipples at a time, pulling and releasing them in tandem. The cows were outside in an enclosed area, except when it rained and for milking. When a cow seemed about to give birth, we would remove her from the rest of the herd. During birth, the two front legs of the calf would appear first; we would rope them and pull. Normally this was enough, and the calf would come out covered in blood, liquid and afterbirth placenta, which the mother would lick, and after an hour it would stand up, a little shaky. Sometimes we needed help and my mother would run to the neighbours – birth time was tense: will it go ok? will it be male or female (female preferred)? There were flies and mosquitoes around the cows always; they would hit them with their tails but in the process often hit us, tail covered with manure, so when we were milking, we would tie the tail to one of the cow's legs. Cows could also kick the bucket into which the milk was directed, so we would hold the bucket between our knees. After some years, again like other people in Shafir, my father bought an Alpha Laval milking machine to assist. Nearly every day I shared in cleaning the shed; we would stand deep in smelly dirty manure, wearing wellies. While living in the moshav, I did not smell the manure but once I moved away it hit me whenever I returned. I mentioned this to my mother, who insisted I was imagining it, as she did not smell anything. Much later, towards the end of her life, when she finally agreed to move to an old age home and made her first and only return to Shafir after living away, she had to agree that I was right about the smell.

Obviously, we did not have sex education when I was a child, but we were exposed to the facts of life early. Cows and humans are not exactly the same, but we knew that the bull had to have sex with a cow for the cow to become pregnant, although usually our cows became pregnant through artificial insemination. The process was carried out by the vet, and we would observe to see when a cow's behaviour grew different. She would jump on the other cows and have something like a period which lasted a few days each month; it was only during these days that she could conceive. We would either take her to a bull we sometimes had or to a bull owned by the moshav for procreation purposes or book the vet. The vet cost money but the result was better calves. In the early years, if a male calf was born, he would be sold within weeks; later we would keep male calves for a year. Cattle are sexually mature by age one, males just before, females just after; so once a male calf reached that age, we sold him for meat. I hated this part of our life, the meat merchants and process of dealing with them. My father was not good at it and even as a child I could see that the merchants played games to push the price down, a problem compounded because we were usually desperate for money. The most common game was for one merchant to offer x per kilogram, which was low, then have another appear to offer even less, making the first offer the best option. No other merchant would come: they cooperated between themselves. Once my father agreed a sale, the merchant would take the bull to a place in the centre where there was a weighing machine and leave it there for hours without food or water so its weight would go down. I came to stand guard to ensure that no foul play occurred. The meat merchants were usually unpleasant people; sorry, but I really disliked them.

The work was hard on my parents, and at the age of nine or ten I started to be the one who took the milk to the dairy in the evening. I used a small hand-pulled cart; the dairy was about five hundred meters away but the first 100 meters near our home was a dirt road and, in winter, it was muddy and I had to use all my strength. Even the asphalted part of the road often had mud on it. I did not want to use the mule, as it meant that the poor animal would be shackled for hours in harness to cart and I would have to free him after delivering the milk, a tedious and time-consuming job. I wanted to be free to play with friends, so I always was the first person at the dairy. Everyone else came with horse (or later tractor) so there was a ramp to make it easy to transfer the heavy milk churns (made of steel), but I had to carry them up the stairs. I learned to read Hungarian since the dairy was a place everyone went to and its notice board had all the important information such as the vet's visits, water stoppages, security issues, etc. I had to report to my father what the announcements were.

Over the years my parents became more and more dependent on me, not only for work. When my mother wanted something, she used to ask me to ask my father for it – it had a better chance of succeeding than if she asked. My mother used to say that I inherited her good genes and my father's good genes; on the whole I agree with her comment but there is much room for improvement.

There was only one family who left Shafir (for South America) and to the amazement of everyone, came back to live there years later. Their name was Cohen, and they made some money abroad and invested it back into farming in Shafir. There was a joke going round: how do you make a small fortune in Shafir? Answer: by starting with a big fortune. It was also said that most farmers put manure into the ground and got out gold, but Mr Cohen put gold into the ground and got out manure.

One of the other Kleins married someone whose husband had died in the War of Independence while she was pregnant, and Klein adopted the child. They had more children but very tragically one of them was killed years later in a terrorist attack.

When I was eight or nine, there was an invasion of locusts in Israel. I believe we were warned because everyone got out with pots and pans and waited in the field planning to make a lot of noise in hope that this would frighten them away. When the locusts arrived, they turned day into night – there were so many that they blocked the sun. No matter how much noise we made, they ate anything green. When they had finished eating everything, and I mean everything, they flew/jumped away to the north. Locusts are kosher and many stayed behind, but we did not eat them.

LIFE AS A CHILD

As children we played a lot; football was popular but there was no proper pitch or grass, all that was needed was a ball. Another popular game was Degel or flag: each team had a small circle with a flag in it deep in the opposite half; the aim was to run through that half to the circle, which was your territory, and return with the flag to your own half without being touched by one of the opponents (they could not touch you while in the circle); if you were touched on their ground, you were frozen and could be unfrozen only by a touch of someone from your own team. There was also Machanayim or camps, played mainly at school: two teams were opposite each other within two marked spaces, with one child of each team at the back of the opponents' team; the aim was to throw a ball and hit someone from the opposing team; if this succeeded, the one who was hit was out; if the ball was caught by someone in the opposing team, the ball moved to them, and the team that ran out of players first lost. The most basic game was Tira: all that was needed was a stick or something like a bat held by the player and a small piece of wood on the ground; the player would bat the edge of the wood to make it jump and then try to hit the wood again in the air to make it fly as far as possible; if the piece of wood was caught, the batter was out and the catcher had the next go; the winner was the one who hit the piece of wood furthest. Other games were machboim, or hide and seek, and simanei derech, or find the treasure. In later years we would play table tennis and basketball, games which required the moshav to spend money. The teams for Degel and Machanayim were mixed boys and girls. The girls also played something called class, jumping on little boxes marked on the ground. I was reminded recently that we used to compete as to who would be the best in guessing the time: none of us had watches. In the early years, apparently, I was the best. Sometimes we went to the main road on Saturday, taking a dead snake which we tied to a thin rope. We would run on the road, pulling the snake behind us so it looked as if the snake was chasing us. When a car stopped to help us, we would shout 'Shabbat, Shabbat...' and run away.

I have two photos from kindergarten. In both, Rafi and I are standing near each other. We also used to play with Binyamin Yosovitch, who was nearly a year younger. This was, he told me years later, because his mother wanted him to be friends with Rafi and me. Our house was nearest to the kindergarten; when the time came that there were no young children in the moshav, the building was changed to a library, and I was glad to live so close to it. I remember from those early days that we used to learn mainly from Rabbi Wolner, who was the rabbi of the moshav until he became the chief rabbi of Ashkelon but kept in contact with Shafir. We studied in the synagogue built of wood, which was at the other end of the centre away from the kindergarten. For some reason I liked studying in those days.

The kindergarten was needed for only fifteen years because of the Holocaust. As mentioned, all members of the moshav were from Hungary and Czechoslovakia; therefore every adult was a survivor. Most of the children were born during the ten years 1946 to '56, as children born earlier would have been killed. There was only one child born during the war, Rafi's elder brother. It was the same story at the other end of age spectrum: only four families had grandparents. One lived in Shafir, two in Jerusalem; as for the fourth, I don't remember where she lived. The age of most of the survivors, when liberated, ranged from late teens to mid-forties. The Nazis murdered the old and the young: they wanted living Jews as slaves only.

Many of the adults had some physical effects because of the Holocaust, but I recall only one who was clearly affected mentally. Looking back, I know that all survivors and their children were and still are affected. Some adults talked about what had happened; some did not. Our parents were overprotective and fed us too much. Food was important and my mother always made hot food even when conditions for cooking were difficult. We children knew that our parents had suffered and generally were good children, helping and even, one can say, trying to protect them. We matured at a young age and did not experience typical teenage rebellion because we did not want to make life more difficult for our parents. Also, we had responsibilities on the farm from a young age and did not need more excitement. I suppose if you know how to use a gun for real when you're thirteen, that's enough. I did have a symbolic rebellion in not eating potatoes, which my parents loved, and my mother had to cook me something else.

As mentioned, my mother was pregnant more than once after I was born but miscarried. Every child is special to his parents, but for my parents I was a miracle, not only because they had lost most of their families but also the failed pregnancies. I was an only child, which is difficult even in normal circumstances, but much more so in our case. One had to be extra careful not to be injured and to be around and available. It also meant that I had to find ways to entertain myself; there was no television, so I spent a lot of time reading whatever I could find. I think being an only child also resulted in me having a overdeveloped imagination. Holocaust survivors generally showed little emotion, but my mother was to some extent different and tried too often to hug and kiss me; I would push her away. Now, of course, I regret it, but I did not want to be different from the others. My father never told me what to do or not to do; I saw what he did and just followed. I knew when he was mischievous; for example, Zvia asked him once 'How does the mule know where to go?' My father's reply was that every morning he whispered into its ear the plan for the day. The truth was that one pulled the reins gently in the direction in which you wanted the mule or horse to turn.

There was no school in the moshav or anywhere near it, but next to the kindergarten was a long hut that became one. It was divided into two, half for the year above me, half for my year. I remember first meeting the children brought over from Massuot Yitzhak; most of them were blond. As far as I recall, we all instantly got on. I don't remember when the children from Zrachia, with immigrants from Morocco and Iran, joined us, but it must have been about the same time. Our teacher, Bilhah, walked over through the fields from the neighbouring kibbutz, Ein Tzurim. Both Massuot Yitzhak, which was not a kibbutz but moshav shitufi, hybrid between a moshav and a kibbutz, and Ein Tzurim were established by those who survived defeat by the Arabs during the 1948 War of Independence. As the school and kindergarten were near home, my mother would walk over during breaks to give me food and milk – very embarrassing.

There were two wells from pre-1948 in Shafir; both were similar, large, round and deep; neither was used by the moshav. One, at the end of our field, was where we threw rubbish; eventually it was totally full – a few years ago I tried to locate it but there was no sign of it. The other was near the entrance to the moshav and had a large mulberry tree near it. As children we risked our life to pick the fruit, even from branches hanging over the well.

CREATION OF SCHOOL

Again I have to praise the visionaries who created the moshavim. By the second school year, a new school was created on a small hill between various moshavim and kibbutzim in our area. A row of four classrooms with separate toilets made of brick was built; also two huts, one for teachers, the other for administrative use. The walls of the classrooms on the west side had very large windows but there were no windows on any other walls; they would have made the rooms too hot in summer. The school expanded every year, new buildings being added, and eventually even a laboratory was built; trees, grass and flowers were planted, making the place attractive. In the third year children from Kfar Achim joined us. We were taken to and from school by lorries with ladders in back that slid under the chassis and benches that could fold up when not in use. The body of the lorry was covered with a tarpaulin, which was usually rolled up at the sides to let air in. The school was a religious and we started the day with prayer. The majority of pupils were Ashkenazi but when a Sephardi boy took the service we followed the Sephardi nusach or text. Israeli society is made up of people from many different places: Sabras or cactus, those who were born in Israel (prickly outside, sweet inside) and immigrants from other countries and cultures. Schools were meant to be the first stage of Kur Hahituch, or the melting-pot, to develop a unified culture and new identity. The second stage was army service, which had more success.

The hill where our school was had been until 1948 home of an Arab village called Sawafir. By the time we came, there were no buildings, only trees, mainly Eshel or tamarisk and palm; there were also some old grenades and explosives. One boy was wounded when he found such a device. The area slightly south and west of Sawafir had seen fierce fighting during the War of Independence, and the invading Egyptian army had reached just northwest of Shafir, where Ashdod is today, forty kilometres from Tel Aviv. The places of fighting near Shafir were the ex-British police station called Yoav – one can still see bullet holes on its wall – kibbutz Negba with its collapsed water tower, Nitzanim and hill number 69. Nitzanim and hill number 69 were captured by the Egyptians, who took 105 Israelis prisoner.

Our school was between two army bases, Kastina & Julis, built by the British (I think) and not far from two air force bases, Tel Nof and Chazor. We often had military planes above and were able to identify them by the sound. As a child, I witnessed two of them crash. The first happened when I was in year three: a light plane flying over the school went down nearby and the two pilots were killed. We were not allowed to leave class for a while, as ammunition was exploding. We learnt that the pilots could have saved themselves by parachuting, but the plane would have crashed into the school, so they lost their lives steering away from us. The other accident was a few years later, during school holiday. A fighter plane crashed in the fields of the moshav. I saw it happening and rode my bicycle to the point where it came down, arriving at about the same time as some military vehicles. Burnt parts of the plane were scattered around, still smoking. I and other onlookers were told to leave; again ammunition was exploding.

My head is full of memories from school. During the second and third years, our teacher was Emanuel Carlebach, who lived in Massuot Yitzhak and was a member of the famous Carlebach family. He had a beautiful voice, like that of his well-known cousin, Rabbi Shlomo Carlebach. Ordinary prayers were led by a pupil but during slichot, or penitential prayers, they were led by Emanuel; still today I can hear his voice and tunes in my head. Later he was appointed headmaster, which was no surprise as he was so good. We had other teachers, but I remember only Gila who was from Jerusalem and not a great teacher, so we were not always on our best behaviour. Once she burst into tears in front of the class; we were embarrassed but not sorry. Around this time Shafir and Kfar Achim had a big influx of new members who had escaped from Hungary after the failed revolution of 1956. As each year was divided into two classes, it was decided to split the classes based on ability; each name was called out and directed to the better group or the not-so-good one; it was, I remember thinking at the time, a bit shaming. Anyway, I was in the better class and during the seventh and eighth years our teacher was Tova Ilan, from Ein Tzurim. Tova was brilliant. She taught us bible, literature and history, the last two not my favourites until she came. We called our teachers by their first names and even nicknames, and relationships were informal. Generally, we had two types of teachers: local ones who were very good and those who came from other not-so-close-by places who were, in most cases, less good, some even bad. I assume the less good teachers could not get a job near where they were living, so we in this remote place got them. Although a religious school, our classes were mixed, boys and girls; the red line was no mixed seating at desks and separation at prayers and sports. When the year above me finished eight years of elementary school, a high school was started, and Tova became headmistress of it. I always liked her very much. Later she moved to the national stage and took part in creating Meimad or Dimension, Hebrew acronym of Medina Yehudit Medina Democratit or Jewish State-Democratic State, a moderate religious party, and became a member of the Knesset. She died in 2019, aged 89, and obituaries in the national papers were full of praise. I agreed with every word. While looking through old papers for this memoir, a small hand-written note fell out; it was from Tova telling me that I did not do well in a grammar exam, I would have to study during the holiday and she was going to test me again. The last time I saw her was fifteen years before her death. I'm upset I did not see her more recently. Somehow I'd always thought of her as closer to my age.

In general, girls were better pupils than boys; the girls wanted to study while we boys enjoyed playing more, and sometimes we would miss class in order to do so. On the northwest of the school's perimeter was a lake; it had water in winter, and we used logs of fallen trees as boats. The best at this was Michael Shtekler who loved being outdoors and was not good at studying. In fact, some teachers gave up on him and on another boy from Zrachia called Yitzhak something, though the teachers called him Yitzhak avir, or air, as he was invisible in class. The south border of the school was a branch of the Lachish River, the town Lachish being mentioned in the Bible. In summer it was easy to cross but not always possible in winter. In one of our playing and running sessions at school, I fell and could not step on my left foot; nothing was visible, but I could not walk. I don't know how I got home, but for the next few days I was in bed with pain and no improvement. During this time Yossi and Binah, twins living two houses away from us, had a birthday party. As I could not go, their father came and carried me on his back. Eventually, I was sent to Kupat Cholim (many called it Kaput Cholim – broken sick) or medical centre in Rechovot, an hour's bus journey away. I had an x-ray and was operated under local anaesthetic to remove a thorn from a branch of palm tree embedded in my leg just above the heel. I still have a scar from the operation. The thorn was so big that, when it was shown to me, I thought it was one of the medical instruments. What happened is that when I'd run over a palm branch which had fallen off the tree – we had many of them – my right leg, lifting, pushed the branch towards my left foot in front and the sharp end of the branch broke as it entered my leg, so nothing was visible.

At some stage during the summer, a person started to come to the school and moshav carrying a big ice box on a bicycle selling ice lollies. We called him gazlen or robber but really, he was trying to make a living in difficult conditions. I remember that he sweat most of the time.

Since we were in an agricultural environment, we studied the theory of agriculture and every two pupils had an allotment to grow vegetables. My partner was Yssachar Kutash from Kfar Achim. Boys also had carpentry lessons, and I think girls had sewing and/or cooking lessons – politically incorrect today. I remember the school as a carefree life; it was much easier than work at home. For example, as each family had use of water on alternate days only, we had to maximise its use, so on the days when we had use of water I got up before six, went up to the field, turned off the sprinklers my father had turned on earlier, moved them one line up or down and turned them on again; the original pipes were heavy as they were made of iron, but those we bought later were made of aluminium, therefore lighter. After that job was done, I would run home, kick off my wellies, push my feet into my sandals without doing them up, drink fresh warm milk and grab something to eat on my way to the place where the lorry picked us up after it picked the pupils from Zrachia. Radio programmes in those days started at six a.m.; what I liked was that they started with singing 'mah tovu ohalecha...' or 'How goodly are thy tents...' then reciting the relevant daily psalm that the Levites would use in the Temple; only afterwards came the news. There may have been something similar from the rich Jewish tradition at the end of broadcasting, but I would have never been up so late. I do know that, once TV was introduced, the day's broadcasting would end with 'psuko shel yom' or 'the daily verse; I used to hear it from neighbours when I lived in town. I don't remember spending much time doing homework; in fact, I remember the opposite. I often did not do homework; sometimes I did it on the ride to school or during breaks, but I did not copy from others. I was caught many times and had to get my parents to confirm that they were aware that I had not done my homework. During boring lessons, I lost interest, sometimes reading a book, holding it under the desk, or drawing in my exercise books. Most of us did not cheat in exams; there was no point really. The teachers knew us well and, if one of the able pupils got a bad mark, the teacher might enquire what had happened. Similarly, if a not so able pupil got a very good mark the teacher might enquire what had brought about the surprise. Not cheating stayed with me for life and helped me at university. As in all schools, we had plays. I was not a good actor, and my mother made the outfits I had to perform in. In one play I messed up my lines: I was an Arab who was supposed to reply to a question that 'my horses and my wives are well' but I said it the wrong way, first my wives, then my horses.

At one point the school introduced tilboshet achida, or uniforms; luckily this did not last long, as it was a burden for our parents both financially and practically. The start and end of breaks was signalled by the shamash, or caretaker (Moshe Zuszman), banging a piece of metal on a disk that used to be part of some agricultural equipment; in time, an automatic electric system was installed. The school eventually created a sports ground for running, long jump, high jump etc.; it built a basketball ground, and basketball became our favourite sport, even at the expense of lessons. We were lucky that the sports ground was on the northeast slope of the hill, relatively far from the classrooms and more importantly from the teachers' room. In secondary school, we created a kind of club, which we called 'the yawning president'. I was president of the club, but the most active member was Israel Nedivi. In those days I was also called 'the genius'. Obviously and unfortunately I was not and am not a genius, but sometimes I would say things that were not expected or straightforward; also sometimes I was asked to answer a homework question which I had not prepared, and I would reply as if reading the answer from my notebook, making it up as I went along. It is true that I was good in gemmarah, part of our religious studies, and in the first year of high school yeshiva, I was put to study it with the year above. The one thing I will accept is that I had, and to some extent still have, a good memory. When my mother's friend Alice asked me to help her son, a few years younger than I, with grammar, I said I was not so good at it, but she said that her son was clever, which was true, and only had some blockage that needed to be opened, so I agreed, and she was right. Because I had to teach it, I looked at grammar more deeply for the first time, seeing its logic and beauty. While helping Ilan, her son, I helped myself even more, and some of what I taught him, who became an engineer but unfortunately died in his early forties, is still with me. I had a similar experience teaching gemmarah to Avraham Levinger during our final school year; he remembers and mentions it still. I don't remember that anyone's background made a difference at school, but the children from Massuot Yitzhak were clearly better off than the rest. They had tuition after school, and all of them spoke Hebrew all the time; most of the adults had not gone through the Holocaust as they had come to Israel before the war.

There were quite a few pupils of my generation who did not do well at school; some even did badly, though some children of these not-good pupils did well, even very well. I put it down mainly to different circumstances between my generation and the next. As life improved and more resources became available to cater for varying needs in education, no one was left out in the way some of my generation had been. The children of those who arrived in 1956 did not know Hebrew but, as far as I remember, they, or at least most of them, adapted quickly.

I sometimes missed out on activities arranged by the school. In at least one year there was a kaytana, or summer camp, which I decided not to go to in order to save my parents the cost and help with the farm. I regretted not going: most of my friends went and came back with great stories. Years later in high school, the class was going to help with archaeological excavations; at the same time, we needed to dig a new hole for the toilet. I decided one digging would be enough and did not join my friends. Again, I regretted it, as I missed not being with them.

On 28 November 1955, an article appeared in *Haaretz* newspaper about our school, which was apparently first of its kind in Israel. *Haaretz* called the school 'a revolutionary experiment'. What was special was that it was for a number of moshavim, rather than each moshav having its own small school, where often two years would be combined into one class. The number of pupils in the school at the date of the article was sixty-one. This type of school became the norm in rural Israel, and eventually, when I graduated, our school had more than a thousand pupils.

with mule and hay cart

CHILDREN FROM NEARBY MOSHAVIM AND TIULIM

Massuot Yitzhak was, as I've said, a moshav shitufi, or partnership moshav. It was not a common type of moshav and, in my opinion, took the best from a moshav and a kibbutz. The children lived with their families, the families drew a monthly sum from the community, the sum was based on the number of family members and each family could do what they wanted with the money. All assets were owned by the community and the members worked in all different aspects of agriculture, some with cows, others with chickens and so on. Massuot also had hired labourers, and it diversified, for example producing taarovet or fodder for animals. Massuot and Ein Tzurim were originally built (1943-47) in Gush Etzion on the road between Jerusalem and Hebron. They and the two other kibbutzim, Kfar Etzion and Revadim, were under siege during the build-up to the end of the British mandate and Declaration of Independence on Friday 14 May 1948. Children and some mothers were evacuated in time; thirty-five fighters sent to help the kibbutzim under siege were killed and their bodies mutilated. We all grew up on the stories of Gush Etzion, as told by people who had fought there. Without going into detail, the first kibbutz to fall was Kfar Etzion and most of its remaining members, over one hundred, were massacred by the Arabs after surrendering. The other kibbutzim surrendered the next day under protection of the Red Cross; two hundred and sixty people were taken prisoner, paraded through Arab towns and eventually taken to Jordan. We were told that, had Gush Etzion not existed and fought, it is likely that not only East Jerusalem would have fallen to the Jordanians but all of Jerusalem. Revadim was the only non-religious of the four kibbutzim.

I don't remember that I was jealous of the children from Massuot; on the contrary, we were close friends, in my case particularly with Yitzhak Weisz (today Itzik Livneh) and Israel Nedivi. They stayed on weekends at my home and I stayed in Yitzhak's. I don't remember staying with Israel; I think I was shy of his pretty younger sister, while Yitzhak had two younger brothers and no sisters. From a young age boys in Massuot drove tractors through the fields to avoid the police to visit us in Shafir, and they taught me how to drive. Most of the children in the moshavim were very independent and responsible from a young age; we had to be, as our parents worked so hard. The gap between Shafir and Massuot was evident also in our tiulim or trips. I liked the annual Tiul: a lorry would pick up all the children of the class from the various moshavim and drive to wherever we were heading. The teachers had the headaches; we brought blankets (the children from Massuot had sleeping bags) and food, per a list given to us by the teachers. This list sometimes gave our parents a headache too, as it was in Hebrew and parents sometimes packed a wrong item; for example, we did not know what shkedei marak was (a replacement of soup croutons); also, the Zorchania or shop in our moshav did not stock everything. We used to sleep on the floor of classrooms in schools round the country or outside under the sky. This was fun for us, even if uncomfortable; we used to spray each other with toothpaste, which was difficult to remove. The trips took us all over and included long walks. If I have to single out one trip, it has to be to Masada. We used to sleep on the ground at the eastern foot of the mountain in Nachal, or river, Arugot. Sleeping outside is not like sleeping in a five-star hotel but most nights in Israel you see thousands of stars. We were woken up at two or three in the morning and started the climb on what is called Shvil Hanachash, or the snake pass. The very early start was for two reasons; to avoid the heat and to enable us to see the sun rise over the mountains east of the Dead Sea. We carried water with us as there was no water on Masada in those days. Today most people take the cable car and reach the top of the mountain in a few minutes. I'm not sure if the effect and the long-term memories are the same as for my generation. The heroic stand against the

Romans by Jews nearly two thousand years ago, and then committing suicide rather than being captured, added to the significance of Masada.

I want to mention Zeadat Yerushalayim, or the Jerusalem march, I took at about age sixteen. Zeadat Yerushalayim is a nationwide annual event in spring, when thousands march from the west up to the hills. Adults march for four days from kibbutz Hulda and youth for two days from Beit Shemesh; as an adult in army service, I marched three times. But when I was sixteen our camp was near Beit Shemesh, and it was easy to walk, as it was a cloudy day. At the end of the first day we got back to our small tents (three pupils in each) and were told to prepare for rain by digging around them. With me were Yitzhak Weisz and Israel Nedivi, none of us very obedient, so we did nothing. It started to rain, and water was coming into our tent, but the rain got very heavy and, no matter how prepared one was, everyone got wet and the tents collapsed. The organisers had to find shelter for thousands of pupils. Everyone walked, in heavy rain, to the town of Beit Shemesh; many were put up in schools and even the bakery and cinema. Our group was directed to a new school, but we were left waiting outside in the downpour as the caretaker would not agree to let us in, all wet and muddy. Eventually, late in the evening, he was ordered by the mayor to open the school, and I and others from my class were put into a new laboratory. We could not sleep as we and all we had was totally wet and full of mud. Someone let out the lab's white mice, and they ran around adding to the confusion. The next day we were all sent home, even though the rain had stopped.

Kfar Achim was similar to Shafir except that many there were not religious. Kfar Achim, or the brother's village, is named after the two Guber brothers who were killed in the

War of Independence; they and their parents became a symbol. I don't know what school the children from Kfar Achim went to before joining Shafir, but all the children joined our school, even the non-religious. Years later Kfar Achim gave an option to children to choose a religious or non-religious school. The two most famous children to come from Kfar Achim are the senior Likud party minister Israel Katz and the retired Chief of Staff and Prime Minister in waiting, Benny Gantz. Both studied in Shafir: Katz's elder sister, Tikva, was in my class, while at some stage Gantz moved to another school. The children who came to us from Zrachia were of a very different background, from Morocco and Iran. From time to time there was tension in Zrachia between members who originated from one country or the other. I don't recall bonding with anyone from Kfar Achim or Zrachia, only with children from Massuot. I hope the fact that I did not bond with anyone from Kfar Achim is proof that my failure to bond with anyone from Zrachia was not due to the racism of Ashkenazim feeling superior to Sepharadim. There were marriages between the children of Shafir and Zrachia, and over the years many from Zrachia moved to live in Shafir. Ester Itzkovitz from Shafir married Danny Dadon from Zrachia, and during my army years I was friendly with Danny who was then a civilian working in the military. I do believe that some of the older generation in Shafir did feel superior to the Sepharadim. Today Shafir has two synagogues, the old one Ashkenazi and a new one Sephardi. Ein Tzurim had younger members so there were no children my age, but anyway later the children from Ein Tzurim went to school in kibbutz Yavneh, near Gedera, as kibbutzim did not want their children to mix with children not from a kibbutz.

LIFE IN SHAFIR

Since all members of Shafir were from the ex Austro-Hungarian empire, certain surnames were common. Klein was one, and to differentiate between the various Kleins, Friedmans, Browns, Shwartzes, Weiszes etc nicknames became useful. One Klein became Ambulance Klein as he was the ambulance driver, another was Barbinosh Klein as he made shaving powder called barbin. My father did not have a nickname, he was just Klein. One Brown was Dily, or mad in Hungarian, though he was not mad at all; his father was Orag, or old Brown. There was Nejash Shwartz, or Shwartz number four in Hungarian, and one Shwartz was called Cigan or gypsy. Cigan Yoshka and his attractive wife Sosi were among the younger generation in Shafir and had more energy than most – my mother used to say they drank strong coffee – and had three attractive daughters. I really knew only the eldest, Yafa, who was two years younger than me. Yoshka was full of life and would sing and dance – no wonder he was called the gypsy. Later in life, he had many ponies and would go with them to fairs and make a living charging for pony rides. Once married with children, whenever I visited my mother over Shabbat, I would take my two young sons to ride on his ponies.

Another person who knew how to sing and dance was Mondshein; one would not realise that he had been frozen during the Holocaust and lost use of half of his lungs. My mother also had a very beautiful voice; I'm angry with myself that I did not record her singing – I would love to listen to her and play her to her grandchildren and great-grandchildren. Once we had electricity, she would always listen to the radio but not always pick out the words correctly; this did not stop her from singing all the new songs she heard. There was a programme called Chipus Krovim, or Searching for Relatives, but I can't remember if either of my parents listened to it. My mother also listened to radio on Shabbat and sewed on Shabbat saying that God would not mind if she had some pleasure. She strongly believed in God (did it help her to survive the Holocaust?) but did not think gentle activity for pleasure was a sin. I would run home from synagogue ahead of my father to tell her it's time to stop. The moshav was formally religious and most members actually were religious, but even those who were not came every Shabbat and festival to synagogue and would not do anything in public prohibited on Shabbat.

Even Shabbat was not a rest day for us. On Friday we had to bring double quantities of food for the cows; my father finished with them just before Shabbat as he always started early anyway, but others milked cows into Shabbat. On Shabbat morning milking was the first thing everyone did and only after finishing did we go to synagogue. When we got a milking machine, we put it on a timer on Shabbat so that we did not need to switch it on; it started automatically. Not milking them would have been painful for the cows and, based on zaar baalei chaim, or animal welfare and suffering, it was permitted to milk them. The moshav hired two Arabs who, on Friday evening and Saturday morning, collected the milk from each household and delivered it to the dairy. The Shabbat morning service started at eight and finished before ten. Everyone slept on Shabbat afternoon. We used to have Bnei Akiva (youth) activities on Shabbat. Most people were not interested in a sermon; they wanted to finish prayers as quickly as possible. When young children we played outside the synagogue but at some stage, I don't recall how old I was, we joined in the prayers. It must have been quite young as the prayers seemed very long. I probably was not yet fully fluent in reading as I was unable to keep up with the chazzan, or person leading the praying.

Looking after the cows was slavery: one had to work seven days a week 365 days a year. Even on Yom Kippur, the Day of Atonement, my father would rush after the end of the service to feed and milk them before eating anything himself; my mother took food for him while he milked. By the way, after neilah, the final prayer of Yom Kippur, one has to recite Arvit, the evening prayer; it was always recited by the same person, Shwartz number four, as he was fastest. We had to work outside on terribly hot days and also in rain. If I did not have to be outside, I liked to look at the rain through the window: I was so happy I could stay inside. Some members gave up on cows; one was Mr Shtark whose eldest daughter, Ester, was in my year. Ester had three siblings and we played together a lot. Mr Shtark became a tractor driver and tried to do additional jobs on the side. He had some beehives and gave me my first paid job. I had a stick with a flat rubber flap and would stand near the beehives to ambush the daburim, or large wild killer bees, who flew in great speed to attack the returning hard-working bees carrying nectar, steal their nectar and kill them. For each dead dabur that I brought to Mr Shtark I got paid something very small. I don't remember but I'm sure I was stung many times. Eventually the Shtark family left Shafir for Bnei Brak. Others like Berger, Mermelstein, Latzi Lazarowitz and his brother in law Edo Kerner became drivers. They were relatively young. Mermelstein eventually built up a transport company and seemed quite well off. He had three attractive daughters: Yehudit, my age, Lea and last Vivi. Their mother told me that when we grew up, I should marry Lea who was the adventuress of the three. She used to hitchhike rather than wait and wait for a bus even though everyone thought it was too dangerous. I was more interested in Yehudit than Lea, but either way nothing happened except both Yehudit and I married partners from the UK. There was another mother who would often tell me that once we grew up, I should marry her daughter, but I did not take any notice of her. I know my mother liked quite a few of the girls in Shafir, but she never hinted that she would have liked me to marry any of them.

Ambulance Klein also had three beautiful daughters: Chava, a year older than I; Shosha, a year younger; and Sara, the youngest. Chava, who was a bit of a dreamer, married someone she met at Bar Ilan University; he was from Ramat Gan. Once married, Emma and I also lived in Ramat Gan and saw them a few times. I found the husband unpleasant; they had a child, and he did not treat Chava properly – to me it seemed that he thought he owned her, like a pretty doll, and did not let her speak in company. Chava eventually committed suicide. When my mother told me, I was in shock. Later, when I worked for Bank Hapoalim, I discovered that one of my colleagues was a friend of the husband. The husband and this colleague plus other friends came to the funeral but members of Shafir blocked their way. This sad episode still upsets me even today.

Of various Friedmans, Lily and Latzi, who had no children, came from the same town in Czechoslovakia as my father, and I used to see them a lot. At some point something happened between my mother and Lily, and the close friendship ended; I have no idea why. Then there were the three Friedman brothers. The eldest, Jusi, was the shamash or beadle in the synagogue and every Friday checked the eruv, which was to enable us to carry on Shabbat within the boundary of the moshav. The eruv was a simple metal wire on posts around all the houses, and Jusi's job was to make sure it was intact. A middle brother was called Kishokosh, or the little clever one, and the youngest, Chaim, was responsible for security in the moshav as he was young enough to have meaningful military service.

Our neighbours to the west deserve special mention. Bingy and Vera were much younger, Bingy clever and interesting and active in the moshav's public affairs, Vera pretty. They frequently argued. They had two daughters, Miriam and Sara, both younger than me. I'm sure I saw Vera every day when I was growing up, as my mother was a kind of mother to her. Vera would come to us after she and Bingy had argued and/or to borrow salt, sugar or whatever and ask my mother to explain the news ot her. As Bingy was active in moshav politics, his cows and fields were a bit neglected. After my father died in 1974, my mother would go to them for Friday evenings. When we came to visit, Bingy would take my older son, Ariel, with him on the tractor. Ariel never forgot how one of Bingy's cows ruined his new coat by doing something which is inappropriate to write and splashing it all over. The two families always got on well; I think Bingy was the only one of the older generation with whom I spoke Hebrew, not Hungarian.

Kibbutz Ein Tzurim was better off financially than Shafir and had lots of fruit trees – oranges, apples, grapes, etc. Once the kibbutz finished picking the fruit, there was always some on the trees that had not been financially worth picking, so the women and children of Shafir were invited to go take the leftovers. We would descend on the trees, eat as much as we could and fill bags; on leaving, our bags were weighed and we paid accordingly. Obviously we did not pay for what we ate, and we ate a lot. I remember the fruit was covered with pesticide; often there was thick white stuff on the outside, and there were no facilities to wash it off before we ate. I'm afraid to write down how much unhealthy and possibly even dangerous stuff we ate. We were not careful, partly because in those days one was not aware of the harmful effects of pesticide. My mother boiled milk to have it pasteurised: she would turn off the flame when the milk started to rise but often would be distracted and it would spill over. We used to buy taarovet or fodder for the cow; it came in 50 kg sacks and contained leftovers from food that had been processed and other stuff. The taarovet had a lot of small pieces, dust and broken bits of carob fruit. The carob is sweet, and I used to put my hand into the sacks feeling around until I'd find carob; I'd take it out and eat it without washing it. There was some vegetable that was grown for the cows; I used to cut it open and eat the inside row and give the rest to the cows. I don't remember what it was called but I'm sure it was not meant for human consumption. During most of my life I was, and still am, able to eat anything, and I can't remember the last time I had a stomach upset. Over the years the cows' menu changed, and nowadays it is easier to feed them.

Food, as mentioned, was important for my parents, especially cooked warm meals. This is no surprise given their experience in the Holocaust. We had three cooked meals a day and meat every day, usually twice. The main meal was lunch, not dinner. Until her dying days my mother was worried that I was too thin. When I lived in London, I came every few months for a week to be with her and help out. On arrival my mother would look at me and say, 'You are ill'. 'Why I'm ill?' I would reply, and she would say, 'You are too thin and pale'. During the Holocaust they were able to predict how many days one had to live based on how thin and pale they were. I think my mother believed that fitter was better, and being fat showed that a person had money.

The first time I saw coffee was when, at six or seven years old, I accompanied my mother to visit a relative; I think it was Steiner, the widower of one of my mother's sisters. I was horrified to see our host dirtying the beautiful and pure white milk with some black stuff. We drank tea only if we were ill, tea with lemon and sugar, never with milk. To this day I rarely drink coffee or tea.

The moshav had some fields that were owned jointly by the community, mainly in areas where there were no water pipes and the produce was dependent on rain for irrigation. These fields were called falcha. Also, the moshav had some citrus orchards, and some of us children worked in them picking fruit. We would carry a special bag that could be opened at bottom; we would pick the fruit until the bag was full, walk back from the trees to the gathering area and offload the fruit by leaning over the big crates and opening the bag's bottom. I liked picking grapefruit as the bags filled quickly, and I hated picking lemons as they were small and it took some time for the bag to fill; also, the lemon tree had pricks that would scratch and cut you. Fruit that was unsuitable for sale was disposed of cheaply to members of the moshav; that went on all the years my mother lived there. Once married, I used to take a sack of oranges and a sack of grapefruit back to town after visiting my mother and make fresh juice every day.

We never ate in a restaurant; falafel was the only thing we bought and ate out, either standing or walking. In the early years in Ashkelon the main street had a few falafel stalls; one was called King of Falafel, another Cesar of Falafel, another King of Kings etc. In later years, once the nearer Kiryat Malachi was developed and had its own falafel stall, we rode bicycles there, especially after the last day of Pesach.

The translation of the name Kiryat Malachi is Los Angeles, but we called it Kiryat Meluchlachy, or the dirty town.

Despite the devastating effect of the Holocaust, there were a number of brothers and/or sisters living in the moshav. The largest in number were the Tzeizlers; three brothers and a sister. The sister's husband himself also had sisters (two) in Shafir. Bingy had a sister and her husband had a brother, all in Shafir. With time, children also joined their fathers. These families and other families created mini-clans with common interest, for example, in the elections to the committees that ran the moshav. Sometimes it became complicated; for example, Bingy and the brother-in-law of his sister were in the same 'party'. The moshav was such a close community that there were no secrets; everyone knew what was happening in everyone else's kitchen and even bedroom. Not everyone was happy or comfortable with so little privacy. Over the years, one heard rumours of affairs both at the moshav and at school. It is a fair assumption that like in all human groupings, there were affairs. I'll not go into more details as I don't have facts.

At some stage newspapers in Hebrew started to be sold in Shafir. Only the weekend paper was available at first, sold by Tova Cohen from my year. She had learning difficulties and I don't recall her at school after elementary years. There were two more children with problems: one was Avrum Yitzhak, who had no siblings, and Bingy was appointed his guardian; the other was a younger girl whose name I don't remember. I started to buy *Maariv*, one of two daily afternoon papers; it had quite a few writers originally from Hungary. Foremost was Ephraim Kishon (Kishhont), who was brilliant; as soon as I got the paper, I'd look for his column. He started to write in Hebrew even before he'd mastered the language and used some Hungarian phrases, which then became acceptable in Hebrew. Kishon became known for his ironic but loving portrayal of day-to-day life in Israel. Yitzhak Weisz also liked Kishon's writing, and we used to compare notes on Sundays in school. Ester Shtark reminded me that I used to read a lot and from time to time burst into laughter ignoring everyone else. Other so-called members of the Hungarian journalist 'Mafia' were Yosi Lapid (Lampash), later deputy prime minister, Zeev and Dosh. Another journalist I liked to read was Jo Finkelstein from the UK. I have no idea why or what I liked in his reporting. Years later in London I met him at gatherings of the Guild of Jewish journalists (Emma belonged to it); he was then a senior journalist on *The Jewish Chronicle*. I started to speak to him in Hebrew, but he told me he did not speak Hebrew. I told him that already when I was a child, I used to read his reporting from the UK in *Maariv* in Hebrew. He was happy to hear that what he wrote was read but told me he wrote in English and it was translated. Emma also became a well-known journalist.

HAESEK HABISH OR THE UNFORTUNATE DEED

I was an avid reader from a young age and, like everyone, I was intrigued by what was hinted at but not openly written. Haesek Habish happened in the summer of 1954, years before I started to read newspapers, but the newspapers, with code words, went on writing about it for more than fifty years. We know today that someone came up with the stupid idea of recruiting Egyptian Jews to put bombs in cinemas and other public places in Egypt to create chaos, blame the Muslim Brotherhood and discredit the Egyptian leadership. The plot was discovered by the Egyptians; two of the secret agents committed suicide, two were hanged and the others imprisoned. The newspapers were not allowed to give details but there was a blame battle between the then defence minister, Pinchas Lavon, and other politicians; also among top-ranking Army officers. Over time the papers gave code names like 'the third man', 'haesek habish', 'the senior officer', 'X' but we ordinary readers did not know the full story. I was fascinated by this, partly because it was top secret but also because it clearly effected, for a considerable time, the leadership of the country. Only years later did the full details come out, and I can't stop thinking how stupid those responsible were. There were a number of official enquiries to find out 'mi natan et hahoraah' or 'who gave the orders'. A few years ago I came to know a cousin of one of the Egyptian Jews arrested. It was a major issue in his life. I also know someone who, as a child, made a match between his teacher and one of the key figures in the sad saga; she became the wife of this 'senior officer'. I was fascinated by the fact that he knew this key figure so well.

THE KASTNER TRIAL

Then there was the Kastner trial, which I remember because my father followed it closely. We used to get the Hungarian language newspaper *Uj Kelet*, or *New East*, but my father was usually too tired to read it. During the trial, however, he waited eagerly for it and read the trial coverage immediately. Naturally *Uj Kelet* had detailed coverage, as it was about events in Hungary during the Holocaust. Greater Hungary, which included parts of Czechoslovakia, Romania, Ukraine and Yugoslavia, had previously close to one million Jews. The Nazis started mass extermination of them late, in

1944. By that time world leaders were aware of systematic, industrial-scale murder of Jews, but nothing was done to stop it. The young Reszo Israel Kastner, a lawyer and journalist, thought the Hungarian Jewish leadership was ineffective; he took the initiative to start negotiations with SS officer Adolf Eichmann, to exchange Jews for money and non-military supplies the Germans were desperate to have. Over a thousand Jews were put on trains to Switzerland and saved. I know one such survivor, who was then a baby. One high-profile passenger was the ultra-orthodox, anti-Zionist Chasidic Satmar Rebbe, Joel Tietelboim, who ironically had objected to his followers leaving Hungary earlier.

In August 1952, someone called Malchiel Gruenwald, who had lost most of his family in the Holocaust, self-published a pamphlet claiming that Kastner had collaborated with the Nazis to save his own family and friends and neglected others by not warning them that they were going to be sent to death rather than resettled. Kastner sued him for libel. I should add here that after Kastner arrived in Israel, he continued his involvement in public affairs and was active in Mapai, the Israeli socialist ruling party. Shmuel Tamir, a brilliant right-wing leaning lawyer, later politician (I visited his home many years ago for a small charity event), saw an opportunity to bash the establishment and ruling party. The trial during 1954 and 1955 directed a light at the Holocaust and especially some dark corners of it. No one remembered any longer that it was Kastner who had sued Gruenwald; it was Kastner who found himself on trial. In his verdict, judge Binyamin Halevy said: 'Kastner sold his soul to Satan'. By now the Israeli establishment realised what Shmuel Tamir had done and the government appealed to the Supreme Court on Kastner's behalf, assigning then Attorney General, Chaim Hacohen, later a Supreme Court judge, to defend Kastner. In March 1957, probably because of all the publicity, Kastner was murdered by zealots before the Supreme Court cleared him from most of the allegations.

It always puzzled me why my father was so interested in Kastner. We were not from Hungary, so I did not see the connection. I never asked why he followed the trial so closely but, because of his interest, I also followed the affair. A few years ago in London I went to a launch of another Kastner biography, this one approved by the Kastner family. The writer praised Kastner and said that in addition to the Jews he saved directly, Kastner extracted Eichmann's agreement not to kill the Jews in a number of camps if the Nazis were defeated. Apparently one of those camps was Mauthausen, where my father had been incarcerated. Did Kastner save my father? I don't know and will never know, but for the first time I understood why my father had followed the trial so intensely.

In late 1994, a play about Kastner was shown on Israeli TV. The writer added a scene, which, as he freely admitted, was not true; in it, Kastner says to one of the real witnesses in his trial that her daughter betrayed her colleagues when she was captured by the Germans in WW2. The daughter was Hannah Szenes, one of the great heroes of the Holocaust. Hannah Szenes was born in Hungary, emigrated to Palestine but volunteered to go back to Europe to help save Jews. She was parachuted by the British into Yugoslavia and captured when she crossed into Hungary. Her mother was still living in Hungary at the time and asked for Kastner's help; she testified at the trial that he ignored her. Hannah Szenes was executed; there are places and streets named in her honour. She also wrote powerful and beautiful poetry, and no one disputes that she was a hero.

The question was, can a documentary play include false facts? The issue came to the Supreme Court and the majority of the judges said 'yes'. In the meantime, in promotional clips, the disputed scene was shown on TV, upsetting the Szenes family and many others. In the end, the scene was withdrawn when the full documentary was broadcast. I was not living by then in Israel, but as with anything to do with Kastner I followed the story. For me Kastner, who was apparently clever, charismatic and handsome, is complex and controversial; he gave positive affidavits to a few Nazis who stood trial after the war, but he risked his life to save people. I don't want to judge anyone for what they did or did not do in horrific circumstances. Merav Michaeli, Kastner's granddaughter, is now a member of the Knesset for the same party her grandfather was a member of, as it evolved over the years.

THE SUEZ CONFLICT

On 26 July 1956, the charismatic Egyptian President, Gamal Abdel Nasser, announced nationalization of the Suez Canal Company, a joint British-French enterprise that had owned and operated the canal since its construction in 1869. What followed brought about a dramatic change in our lives. The years between 1950 and '56 were difficult in our moshav and in Israel in general. As mentioned, at night Arabs would sometimes walk or ride between Gaza and the West Bank and damage and steal livestock, equipment etc.; more seriously those called fedayeen would kill or injure people living on the route, which usually brought about Israeli retaliation. The border was an armistice line, not a natural border like rivers or mountains; in most places it was marked just by barbed wire with a notice in English, Arabic and Hebrew 'Stop. Border ahead'.

Britain, France and Israel hatched a secret plan: Israel would invade Sinai and advance towards the Suez Canal; Britain with France would volunteer to 'protect' the canal but in practice occupy it. Israel's main representative and negotiator was Shimon Peres, who died only a few years ago. On 29 October of that year, Israel invaded and, after a short war, occupied most of Sinai, stopping sixteen kilometres from the canal as publicly demanded by Britain and France, both of whom sent paratroopers and naval task forces to occupy the canal. World reaction, especially the Arab world, the USA and the then USSR, was furious. On 4 November, the USSR used the opportunity, when world attention was focused on the Middle East, to invade Hungary and use brutal force to put down Hungary's attempt to have democracy and leave the communist bloc. Ironically, this had another effect on us, as will be described, bringing a wave of Hungarian refugees to Shafir.

When the war started, our school closed. Lorries were taken to be used by the army, so we could not be driven to classes. All pupils stayed in their own settlement, with some adults teaching us a little in the same zrif or hut where we'd studied before the school had been built. I clearly recall that we spent most of the time on the swings and generally playing, but we did try to understand what was happening, and we got the story of Israeli paratroopers surprising the Egyptians from behind. I don't recall if we understood anything else. As children, we saw things in a simplistic way: we loved the French, were suspicious and did not know what to make of the British and were angry with the US and USSR. We hated the Arab states. Only a few adults from the moshav were called for military duty, as most of them were too old. Before the war, three crude simple air shelters were built in the moshav, some in the school also. To save cost, they were built mostly above ground and covered with rocks and earth. Eucalyptus trees were planted to hide them; the playground was near one of them. These shelters still exist, but they were never used and are no protection against today's rockets from Gaza; anyway, each house has now its own mamad or 'safe' room.

Under world pressure, Britain, France and Israel withdrew and UN forces were put on the border between Israel and Egypt. For the next eleven years, the border was peaceful, and Israel gained freedom to use the Red Sea. We went sometimes to the border, especially the crossing point where UN officials and diplomats passed in their fancy vehicles. The contrast between before and after the war was incredible: for the first time, we had a near normal life. This changed again just before the Six Day War of 1967.

at the dairy, around 1960

NEW REFUGEES: THE HUNGARIAN REVOLUTION

At the end of 1956, after the unsuccessful attempt to overthrow the Communist regime in Hungary, many of that country's remaining Jews emigrated. Most of them arrived in Israel, with quite a few landing in Shafir as I've said. All the empty houses of families who had left became occupied again and there were many new children of the same ages as the existing children. In order to give these new immigrants something to do, someone, I don't know who, decided to build an extra room and proper bathroom in each house in the moshav; so the new immigrants started their working life in Israel as unskilled builders. Once the work was completed, they downgraded, we can say, and joined the existing members of the moshav as unskilled farmers. Since everyone spoke Hungarian in Shafir, the new immigrants integrated quickly; the children had to learn Hebrew, and some found it difficult, but most of them integrated quickly too. One of them was Shimon Shifer, who became a leading journalist. Because we already had a veranda at the front of the house, our additional room was built at the back. It was built well, and became my bedroom. It had a proper ceiling, proper small if cheap floor tiles and windows with netting to keep out flies, mosquitoes and lizards. Every morning I would open the shutters and see the big cypress trees which marked the boundary between Shafir and Ein Tzurim. In the early years there were boundary conflicts between the two settlements, and I have no idea how they were resolved. Years later the cypresses were cut down, and I miss them. There were also many cypress trees alongside the main road between Ashkelon and Gedera; they too were cut down to make room for a wider road. It all looks so bare now.

THE SHOAH OR HOLOCAUST

I've been using the word Holocaust in this memoir, as it is what is used usually round the world to describe what happened to us, the Jews, in Europe in WW2. I would have preferred to use the Hebrew word Shoah, which means destruction, not only because holocaust also means sacrifice, but for me Shoah captures better what happened. I also have issue with one of the Hebrew words used for survivors. There are two words in Hebrew, one *sordei* shoah and the other *nitzolei* shoah. Both mean survivors but the root of the second word also means 'removed from'. The Holocaust never gets removed from the survivors or their descendants.

Once there were enough children over the bar mitzvah age, we started a minyan or prayer group run by children for children. It was held in the new moadon or club building. For a while one teacher came to help us, both on Friday evening and Saturday morning, walking all the way from the school where he lived, forty-five minutes each way. We always felt embarrassed and uneasy with the Ashkenazi or diaspora accent of our parents; it seemed a symbol of the unhappy past. Israel represented the new Jew fighting for his country, working the land and different from the diaspora Jews who just a few years earlier had been taken like sheep to the slaughter. This was a very significant issue, rarely spoken about openly; and it was not unique to Shafir. Throughout the country, Holocaust survivors were made to feel ashamed that, unlike Israelis, the Jews in Europe had not resisted the Nazis and their local collaborators in significant numbers. On top of this, not everyone believed the horror of what had happened; they just could not accept that human beings could perpetrate such evil. As a child, I could not hear anything about the experiences of my parents. While my father would not speak about them, my mother eventually had no problem talking. It was Emma, who is Sephardi in background and whose family did not suffer death in the Holocaust, who drew my mother out about her experiences. Both my parents died before various projects to document the history of Holocaust survivors started. Like all children in Shafir, I was living totally in the shadow of the Holocaust but not fully aware of it at the time.

This all changed with the capture of Adolf Eichmann by Israeli Mossad agents in Argentina on 11 May 1960. Eichmann was a member of the SS, the Nazi paramilitary corps and became, in effect, executioner of what the Nazis called 'the final solution to the Jewish question' – systematic murder of Jews. Eichmann was smuggled to Israel and put on trial, which lasted from 11 April to 15 December 1961. He was sentenced to death, the only death sentence ever imposed by an Israeli court. On 31 May 1962 he was hanged, and his ashes scattered at sea. The trial or part of it was broadcast live on radio, and at school we listened and discussed it (I don't remember any details). One of our teachers was a survivor, and on Holocaust Memorial Day, which in Israel is 27 Nisan, around the time of the heroic uprising by Jews of the Warsaw Ghetto, he was supposed to speak to the whole school. He stood in front of us, repeatedly trying but being unable to utter even one word. This was the first time I understood a little about the Holocaust, and it was down to a relative stranger to hammer it home. The evidence and stories that came up in the trial changed the attitude of many Israelis to survivors; they no longer looked down on them but began to admire their courage, stamina and determination. Still, there were Jews who did not like the change and saw their own stories and sufferings, for example, in Arab countries, as unjustifiably overshadowed by the Holocaust.

The only person in the moshav clearly mentally affected by the Holocaust was Bingy's sister. She hardly ventured out and we could hear her shouting; her poor husband Leichy was an angel looking after her; they had no children. A few people had visible physical damage, like Aberstark, one of whose arms just hung from his shoulder. He had jumped out of the train deporting him and broken it; not treated, it was damaged for life. My mother's eyesight was another example; she had glaucoma, which went untreated, and her eyes were damaged for life. I don't know if living in Israel during the early years of the state without adequate medical help contributed to the problem, but it surely did not help.

Though I have no memories of being told as a child what my parents went through, I always knew most of what I know today, as we permanently lived in the shadow of it. Both parents had numbers tattooed on their arms, as the Nazis wanted human beings to become just numbers; I'm angry that I never noted theirs down. Another visible thing was that we had many family photographs – grandparents, uncles, aunts, great uncles, great aunts and cousins – but none was alive, so I twigged that something terrible had happened. Zvia's parents survived, as I've mentioned, by escaping to Hungary; they pretended to be unmarried so that, if one was caught, the other would have a chance to survive. They lived in constant fear of being discovered, as an incident will illustrate. One day a woman working with my aunt brought her some flowers; my aunt, not known for politeness, asked what had happened. When she heard the woman reply 'But it is your Saint's day!', her heart sank. My aunt feared she had given away the secret that she was not Christian. Luckily the woman did nothing.

In January 2016, for international Holocaust Memorial Day, I wrote an article for *The Tablet*, an English Catholic weekly, about growing up in the shadow of the Holocaust. Years before, I had been confronted in London by an older Italian half-Jewish friend. 'Why are you not talking about the Holocaust to your teenage children?' she demanded. I was surprised by the question; I'd never thought of talking to my children about it; I'd tried to push the Holocaust away. Later I said to her that I was just doing what my father had done and, more to the point, why inflict this terrible horror and burden on the children. Whenever the subject came up with friends, the most I would say was that I couldn't understand how 'normal' people could be so evil and what had they been thinking when they participated in murdering millions of innocent man, women and children. I tried to read Viktor Frankel's book *Man's Search for Meaning*, published in 1946, and Hannah Arendt's book *Eichmann in Jerusalem: a report on the Banality of Evil* but I could not. Frankel wrote that those who survived were sustained by hope; as hard as I tried, I couldn't believe my father had hope. As for my mother, I don't know, but I accept that it is possible she had some kind of hope. Frankel's book was criticised by many because he indirectly blamed the victims, as if they had only had hope they would have survived. I found Arendt's writing, the little I read of it, too complicated to identify with. What did stick in my mind, but I don't remember who wrote it, was that there was a direct link between Martin Luther, the play *Faust*, Satan and Nazi ideology. Luther dismissed the value of good and free will, Faust sold his soul to Satan (remember the inappropriate comment of Judge Halevy in the Kastner trial) for unlimited power; if Satan rules the world, the 'final solution' is possible. Apparently, Heinrich Heine argued that beneath German spirituality there is barbarism; he wrote the much-quoted phrase 'Where they burn books, they will ultimately burn people'.

There were a few rabbis who said that the Holocaust was a punishment for Jews not being religious or observant enough; this makes my blood boil. They should read the book of Job. As I wrote above, I rarely read books or saw documentaries or movies about the Holocaust, so for me it stayed largely in the background. It moves to the front at unexpected times – for example, whenever I have a medical check-up and, as normal, am asked about family medical history. This simple, routine question always affects me – I'm not going to say: 'Nearly all my family was murdered before I was born'. I'm irritated with myself that too quickly and too often I start to have tears in my eyes. I think that in addition to my tears I also have those that my parents, like most survivors, did not shed when it came to this subject.

To my surprise, after my mother died – my father had died twenty years earlier – something changed; I can add that it changed dramatically. The Holocaust refused to stay in the background; it pushed itself to the front. In a way I felt that, with the death of my mother, the burden had moved on to me. Before I had felt as if the Holocaust was everywhere around me; now it felt as if it were IN me, or, more accurately, I was in it. It was always difficult for me to talk about it; now it became nearly impossible. On our first visit to Czechoslovakia after the fall of Communism (I could not visit earlier because of my Israeli passport), we went to the old Jewish quarter of Prague. Next to the cemetery was the building where the dead used to be cleaned and prepared for burial; now it was a museum. In it were drawings by children from Theresienstadt; below each was written the date when the child was sent to Auschwitz. As we walked further into the hall, I started to have breathing difficulties, tears coming down preventing me from seeing clearly. I had to run out to recover. What had happened was that sometime earlier I'd read a description that made me realise for the first time how victims in the gas chambers died (I can't write it) and now I felt it. Once I recovered, I went back to normal, enough to continue our visit to Czechoslovakia. But it became difficult to go back to normal after my mother died. Even casual mention of the Holocaust on television, by friends or anyone, resulted in difficulty to sleep that night.

One of the most powerful memories from childhood is the synagogue in Shafir on the 10th of the Hebrew month of Tevet. The date is a traditional fast day and was chosen as the day on which to say Kaddish for all those who had perished in the Holocaust, as the exact date of their death was unknown. (Normally Kaddish is said on the anniversary of the death.) As everyone in Shafir was a survivor and the date of death of most victims was not known, everyone said Kaddish on 10 Tevet. It was a very unusual – and I have difficulty finding the appropriate word – phenomenon. Similarly, when on some festivals yizkor or 'in memory' was recited, all the adults participated in the service as all had lost close relatives; only children stayed outside. The tradition is that those who did not lose close relatives went out. As a child, I also went out, even though I had lost my half-sister(s); I don't know if this was because of the rule or because my parents did not want me to know what had happened. Once I mentioned these matters to a neighbour in London, a senior doctor, and he asked whether many people in my moshav suffered from depression. The answer was no, they did not have the luxury to be depressed; they had too hard a life. When I was a young teenager, I was struck by a short prayer on most Shabbatot, which occurs just before returning the sefer Torah, or the

Torah scrolls, to the ark. I thought it may have been compiled after and because of the Holocaust and asked my father if that was so, but he told me it existed already. I found out later that it was written after the first Crusade, 1096-1099, when so many Jews had been killed. The prayer is: 'Father of compassion who dwells on high in His powerful compassion... the holy congregations who gave their lives for the Sanctification of the Name...' I often remember the Holocaust when I say it.

A while ago we had, for a short time, some family therapy. I was surprised to hear from my younger son repeatedly how the Holocaust had affected him. Later we had therapy again for a bit longer, and the therapist, a non-Jew, kept referring to the Holocaust. I did not want this: it was too difficult for me and I thought it irrelevant to what we were trying to achieve, but he was fascinated by the subject and would not let go until the end of our sessions.

I prefer not to travel to Germany or Poland (a big Jewish cemetery), and I don't buy German cars or German-made goods. I don't have a problem associating or being friendly with Germans as obviously anyone living today who was involved in the murder of Jews would be well over ninety. Many people try to deny the Holocaust, a thing I can't understand. Another thing I can't understand is people calling Israelis Nazis. I don't think these two absurdities need detailed discussion, as they are so clearly untrue. Also, people say Israel is a racist country because only Jews have an automatic right to live there but, as anyone can become a Jew regardless of skin colour or background, Israel is not racist. I have never heard an analysis or explanation of the Nazis' behaviour that is adequate; perhaps I missed it, but I think there is no satisfactory explanation. What the Nazis did was absolute and complete Evil; if it helps anyone, we can call it a manifestation of Satan in its worst form. There have been so many man-made tragedies, massacres and genocides since the Holocaust; humanity has not learned.

Jews suffered throughout history. They were expelled from their own country and other places they lived. There were restrictions on what they could do and where they could be. In certain places and times, they had to wear signs to distinguish them from others. For generations, they could not go to universities, which ironically are supposed to be the height of knowledge, openness and liberalism; and once Jews were allowed to go, there were restrictive quotas. The same with law and accountancy firms. Today most people will say that anti-Semitism is unacceptable, but that does not stop them from indulging in it. Much of today's anti-Semitism is channelled against Israel. History shows that singling out a group of people, religion or country leads to disaster. With the collapse of imperialism and rise of nationalism, the state of Israel would have been created even if the Holocaust had not happened. But the Holocaust made the creation of it an immediate necessity.

ENTERTAINING OURSELVES

It's time for more positive comments. Despite the hardship and lack of money, our childhood was a happy one. Everyone was more or less on the same level, so there was little jealousy. In the early years, people did not lock their front door; anyway, there was nothing to steal. As children we ran freely all over the moshav and beyond. My parents had an old bicycle, and I and some friends taught ourselves to ride by falling down and getting up again until we had learned. We were too short to be able to sit on the seat;

nevertheless, we rode even as far as Ashkelon. We must have also used the bus to go to the beach there, which required two buses. The beach in Ashkelon was beautiful, with golden sand for miles and miles. The sea itself was often rough; there was a lifeguard and flags to indicate what was allowed. White flag indicated calm sea, red rough sea but allowed to go in a short distance, black no entry to the sea. We had to be careful of the underwater currents; normally they just interfered with swimming, but once I swam too far and had to use all my strength to free myself from the pull. After the Six Day War an oil pipeline was constructed between Eilat and Ashkelon, and the beaches became less perfect.

At some stage we children started collecting and exchanging empty cigarette packets; our bicycle trips on the main roads helped our collections, as drivers and passengers threw empty packets out of buses and cars. We were always occupied and did not feel we lacked anything. On rainy days, in addition to work, I used to read or go to friends; I remember playing chess and similar games. Most often I would go to Rafi and we used to play cards, his sister Rachel and neighbour Zvika joining in. Rafi's mother used to ask what would happen if both Rafi and I fell in love with the same girl. It never happened; I was too shy and did not have a sister and therefore did not know how to behave with girls and never had a girlfriend. Over the years, I was close to a few girls but Rafi and others were more advanced. Rafi's girlfriend for many years was Shosha, the middle daughter of Ambulance Klein; I liked Shosha, she was lovely, but never imagined us as a couple. It did not help that in early teenage I touched one of the girls and she made a scene. I don't remember what exactly happened: it was with a few of us standing together waiting to go in to see a movie, so it could not have been bad. I think she just wanted to impress her girlfriends and pretend she was 'not interested'. As far as I remember, she was friendly later, but I kept my distance. The episode did not give me confidence about how to behave with girls, even if I believed that one wanted to be close to me. At times I thought that x or y liked me, but I never was certain, and with the religious life we led, I just did not know what I should do, so I did nothing. That does not mean that I was not frustrated, the opposite.

On motzaei Shabbat, or after Shabbat, we used to go to see movies in neighbouring Kfar Warburg, which was established quite a few years before Shafir and therefore (at least in part) more advanced. Edo, who was a driver/owner in the company that took us to school, would drive his lorry there and back, so everyone in Shafir who wanted to go, mainly children, had to pay a small amount to him. As I collected the fare, I did not have to pay. We did not mix with the children from Kfar Warburg – they probably looked down on us – but, as we went there nearly every motzaei Shabbat, we recognised the locals. This gave me quite a dilemma on the day I joined the army, of which more later.

Some of the adults played cards, including Rafi's father and uncle, but not my father. Similarly, my aunt and uncle played in Haifa, originally using cards but later domino size stones. When these stones were shuffled on the balcony of a flat, all the neighbours would hear it. In most buildings the balconies were close to each other, and people spent their evenings there because of the heat. Sometimes Zvia and I played with her parents, but I never took to cards and have never played since. Zvia still has those little stones and, during a recent visit of mine to Haifa, we played again, though she had to remind me of the rules. Zvia also had Lego, which was exciting, but I don't remember anyone in

Shafir having Lego. Some children in Shafir had dominos and chess sets and I think also Monopoly. While in Haifa, I joined the evening walks of Zvia and her parents to the centre of town; we used to walk up to beit hakranot, or the corner house. Part of the walk back was up a steep hill, good exercise, which was the reason for these regular excursions.

TRAPPED IN SHAFIR

Three things converged around the same time: WW2 ended, I was born, and the state of Israel was created; so I saw the world as if it was rebooted, and anything pre-Israel wiped off. This meant that I ignored most things that took place in the last two thousand years or at best looked down on them. This was, as said, notably in regard to the diaspora versus Israel. I was totally uninterested in Czechoslovakia, the country where I was born and my family had lived for centuries. I did not feel claustrophobic living in tiny Israel surrounded by hostile enemies. I did not intend to visit any other country; I felt my ancestors had lived in Israel and it did not matter that most Jews had lived outside for two millennia. At school I didn't participate in English lessons; I did not like the teachers but also I regarded it as a waste of time. I did not believe I'd ever be able to leave Shafir and live in a town. At the age of about sixteen I thought I should learn something practical such as car mechanics, which you could do as an apprentice and earn money, but the school did not agree. Shafir for me was a foreign and alien planet in Israel. During my teens, occasionally I felt trapped in it.

I assumed anyone with a car was rich. I knew only one family who owned a car, my father's cousin Mangel, who had been my mother's friend since childhood. Mangel was a doctor and he and his wife had lived in Israel since the 1930s. When I knew them, they lived at 22 Nordau Boulevard, Tel Aviv. They visited us sometimes; in addition to my aunt and uncle, they were the exception. Once when all three of us, my father, mother and I were working in the fields, I saw two or three people walking around our house, so I returned to it to ask what they wanted. They seemed embarrassed and asked for my parents; I said they were further off in the field. I asked if they were relatives, which embarrassed them even more. They continued to be vague as we all walked to where my parents were. The reason I remember this is because they seemed a little emotional. The two men were brothers of my father's first wife (née Stern). I'm sure my father would have met them in Czechoslovakia after the war, but I don't think they had met since arriving in Israel: they lived in another moshav, called Chemed, near Ben Gurion Airport. After that meeting the families kept in touch. More generally, I felt as if we had leprosy because so few of the family came to visit us. I should have realised that it was quite difficult to get to Shafir by bus. Being accepted or not followed me into adulthood.

NATURE AROUND SHAFIR

The northern boundary of the moshav was the Nachal, or River, Lachish, I already mentioned the southern branch of Nachal Lachish, which was near the school. This was the northern branch. It was much bigger than the southern, but nevertheless also dry in summer. The water level in winter fluctuated between a trickle and a strong flood that swept everything in its path. The river joined the Mediterranean where Ashdod was built in 1956. In the early years of

Ashdod, before there was a proper bridge, a few people actually drowned when trying to cross the river in winter. It was used as a rubbish damp by those living along its route, but we children often went there to play. In winter and spring it was full of flowers, especially red poppies. There were also wild animals: we often heard jackals at night; and there were rabbits, tortoises, butterflies and many birds, some local but also huge numbers which came during migration times. Because of its geographical location millions of birds pass over Israel during migration. There is a difference between me who grew up within nature and still likes to be surrounded by it and Emma who, like many town people, likes to be in town only. Emma does not notice birds, butterflies and similar creatures even if she is looking at them. I also like the sound of nature, birds singing and, unlike in my childhood, now even the noises made by frogs and crickets. Also I like the complete silence one can have in nature. I am able to find my way easily both there and in town and can feel my way in the dark quite accurately.

Early 19th century pilgrims to the Holy Land commented how bare the landscape was, with few trees. This started to change with the arrival of Jews later on in the century. They started to plant trees, and over the years it became a priority. As children, the importance of trees was drummed into us. The Keren Kayemet LeIsrael, or Jewish National Fund, took it upon itself to raise money to enable trees to be planted all over the country. As I was growing up, I could see hills and deserts getting greener and greener.

The River Lachish was also used by Bedouins – Arab nomads, from the Negev, or southern part of Israel. They lived in tents, had horses, camels, sheep, goats and donkeys. They let us ride on the camels and donkeys and would give us tea in small glasses. Half of the glass was sugar and half very strong tea or coffee. The Bedouins stayed weeks or months, then moved on. Barefooted children, boys and girls, looked after the herds. They did not go to school.

We always suffered even inside the house from mice, rats, snakes and other unwelcome creatures. My father used to put DDT around the perimeter. I wonder if that was the reason, years later, for his cancer. We always had cats and dogs; they used to adopt us – once we had given them food, they stayed, but they were never allowed to get into the house. My mother was particularly good to injured animals or those born with defects.

For the first thirty or forty years, most members of Shafir wanted to leave and find a better place to live, but as some of the children of the founders stayed and made Shafir their home the trend started to change. In addition, many of the younger generation from neighbouring Zrachia bought houses in Shafir. Increased demand resulted in increased value and investment. Many houses now are big and attractive, very different from the past, and grandchildren of the founders are living in Shafir. In the case of Avi and Dvorah Werthiemer, for example, both born and bred in Shafir, all their five children remained.

BAR MITZVAH

There were only a few boys who had a bar mitzvah before me; I was the first in my year. Rabbi Deutch, who came to Shafir in 1956 as part of the Hungarian influx, spent a lot of time with me, teaching me the Gemmarah relevant to the subject I was going to give my Drasha or speech on. It was in his interest to do so, to be paid more; my father paid him with chickens and eggs. Regardless, the rabbi did believe that the temple would soon be rebuilt and I, as a Cohen or priest, had to know the relevant laws. I was open to learning and liked the challenge and did well. I can't say the same about the shochet who taught me to read the portion of the Torah which was parashat Shemot, or the first portion to be read from the book of Exodus. The reading had to be done with specific tunes, as per the teamim or notes. Unfortunately, I inherited my father's singing genes, not my mother's. No one can blame my father for being able to sing; he had zero ability at it and so do I. The poor teacher had a difficult time and fully earned his fees, also paid with chickens and eggs. I read the minimum required length of the Torah and the Haftarah and, given my zero talent, did not do too badly, unless everyone was lying to me. Unlike other children, I never read it publicly again. My drasha was much better, despite having a very long one written mainly by the rabbi, his Hebrew corrected by me.

The reading was during a morning service when I also, for the first time, participated in Birkat HaCohanim, or the priestly blessings. The tradition in our synagogue was that the bar mitzvah boy, after his reading, went up to the ladies' gallery – men and women sat separately in our synagogue – to be blessed and congratulated by his mother. The party was that afternoon. There were not enough benches to enable everyone to sit, so I talked to Emanuel Carlebach, the headmaster, and he agreed that we could borrow a number of benches from school. My father hired Israel Rabin, who lived not far away and had a tractor, and on Friday, just after school, they came and loaded the benches onto a platform towed by the tractor to take them to Shafir. The party was in the old moadon, the long wooden hut I mentioned earlier, near my home. I have some photos with the moadon in the background, an unimpressive building with small windows.

Zvia and her parents stayed with us over Shabbat but there was no room for anyone else to stay, so Tibi and his wife Aranka came on Shabbat; they had to hitchhike as there were no buses on Shabbat in Israel. No other relatives or cousins of my parents were invited as it was too complicated. All the food was prepared by my mother, my aunt and some of my mother's friends.

My father bought me the cheapest tefilyn or phylacteries he could find; most of my friends, if not all, received the same. I received presents. My aunt and uncle repaired an old (I think expensive) wristwatch and gave it to me; I wore it every day for a long time until it stopped and still have it; they also gave me some practical items, like socks. Tibi gave me first day stamp covers, which I still have. Other presents were useful handkerchiefs from Rabin and a prayer book with a cover made of tin from Israel Tzeisler, which I still have. I also still have a miniature book of Torah given to me by a cousin of my maternal grandfather. The rest of the presents were mainly books, which was great. Before my bar mitzvah, I remember receiving toys only once, small garden tools. I don't remember why I got them, but I do remember playing with them rigorously. Early on Sunday morning, Rabin and my father returned the benches to school; I helped in unloading them. Emanuel Carlebach arrived, and I introduced him to my father. Emanuel was very happy to meet my father for the first time after being my teacher for six years. My father had never come to parent/teacher meetings as he was too tired; my mother usually came. Some parents in Shafir never went to parent/teacher meetings because, as said, they did not speak Hebrew, only Hungarian. Apparently one teacher grew somewhat cross with the parents not speaking Hebrew. 'You are living in Israel and you should know Hebrew,' he said. A parent replied, 'We don't know Hebrew because we live in Shafir', which was very true. I was told by someone that for those who don't understand Hungarian, when they hear it, it sounds as if the speaker is complaining of stomach upset. Hungarian is not an efficient language; the sentences are long and convoluted. My bar mitzvah memories have stayed with me all of my life.

The first time I used a telephone was during one of my visits to Haifa when I was fourteen or fifteen. It was a public phone, and I was a little afraid of the noisy instrument. Zvia dialled for me the number of someone she wanted either to be a close friend with or the opposite and told me what to say. I spoke very loudly and did not succeed in Zvia's mission. The next time I used a telephone was in the army.

I have some photos Zvia took of my parents with me; I was between fifteen and sixteen and nearly a head taller than my father and a head and half taller than my mother. I think I stopped growing taller at the age of sixteen.

with my parents, aunt & uncle, early 1960s;
mule in the background

RELIGION VS. SECULARISM

Our moshav was part of the moderate religious movement of Hapoel Hamizrachi, or Mizrachi workers. The name Mizrachi is East, indicating Israel, but it is also the Hebrew acronym of Merkaz Ruchani or spiritual centre. While growing up, I did not notice any tension between religion and secularism. My father did not approve of two of the moshav members because, he said, they stole from the community or other members, then gave the money to the synagogue, as if this made stealing permissible. All the children went to the only available local school, which was religious. During elections, the Mizrachi political party in various forms received most of the votes, including, once I was over eighteen, mine, but there were many who voted for other parties. I have my mother's original membership booklet (No. 34761) of Histadrut Hapoel Hamizrachi, or the trade union of the Mizrachi workers; she joined on 9 May 1950 and was a member until she left the moshav.

There were a few who were Charedi when they joined the moshav, among them the Barbinosh Klein family, but they quickly adapted to the Mizrachi lifestyle. Only the rabbi and his family stayed really Charedi; their son, Moshe, was the only male from our moshav who did not go into the army. At times I thought that the youngest daughter, Chaya, might rebel, but she did not; strangely she wanted to shidech or match me with some of her Charedi friends from the orthodox girls' school she went to in Bnei Brak. By coincidence, the strict headmistress of that school was the wife of my mother's cousin, Schmiedel, who started 'Atra Kadisha' or Holy Place, dedicated to protecting burial places unearthed during development works all over the country. He often hit the headlines.

At the end of beit sefer yesody, or elementary school (years one to eight), I and most but not all of the boys in my class went to the newly created (one year earlier) yeshiva tichonit, or yeshiva high school/religious school. The name of the yeshiva was Or Etzion or Light of Etzion, commemorating the four kibbutzim mentioned earlier destroyed in the war of independence. It was built south of the school, just beyond the southern branch of River Lachish in an area being developed as a centre for teachers and employees of the local council. Creating Or Etzion was a visionary move; sixty years later it is one of the leading Bnei Akiva yeshivot in Israel, and a number of its graduates have reached prominence in Israeli life. Back in the early '60s, it had few buildings, and the main studies took place in an old warehouse built of corrugated metal, very hot in summer and cold in winter. The first rosh yeshiva, or principal, was Harav Binyamini; he was a new 'convert' to Chabad, the Chasidic movement, and wanted his pupils to follow it. I still have the prayer books of Chabad that we had to buy, but the more he tried to make us Chabadniks the more anti-Chabad I and a few of my friends became. I admire what Chabad does but did not like the way they worshipped the rebbe. Harav Binyamini left at the end of my first year; in fact, he held the job for two years only. His replacement was the young charismatic Harav Chaim Drukman, still in the job now in his late eighties. My father took me and my belongings to the yeshiva on the mule; among the belongings we had to take were blankets, but we did not have proper ones. My mother travelled to Ashkelon to buy leftover ends of blankets and was planning to sew them together to create a single one, but she could not find leftover pieces of the same colour, so I ended up with a multi-coloured blanket. I did not feel proud like Joseph, who received from Jacob his father a multi-coloured garment, but the opposite: I was embarrassed.

Days started with prayers, followed by breakfast, and the morning was dedicated to religious studies, mainly gemmarah. I liked religious studies, I found it challenging; it was also our history and a source of inspiration. Secular studies took place in the afternoon, and we did not cover all that was studied in a regular high school. The experience was different to what we were used to; there were no girls and we lived in a dormitory. A few girls from our class visited us once at the start of the year but they were told by the yeshiva not to come again. The dormitory rooms were small and uncomfortably crowded with bunked beds, I continued to dislike English lessons and would hide inside a cupboard in my room and read forbidden books using a torch. The food was not great, and I remember someone asking: 'Can we have bread from today?' The answer was: 'Of course, come tomorrow'. There were many pupils from around the country, but the boys from our class were the largest group. New friendships, some lifelong, were formed, including with pupils from South America, who had come to Israel to study. Early in my first year, the yeshiva had a visit from the son of the late highly regarded Harav Kook, himself a prominent and leading rabbi. He made a special blessing when he saw us studying in the big warehouse, which he and other visitors found impressive.

My father got a discount on fees, but he would have paid full price if he had not. I'm sure he was happy that I was studying in a yeshiva, as he had done when my age. I knew he had gone to a yeshiva in Surany but had no information about it. Long after he died, I met the grandfather of a friend of my niece who had studied in the same yeshiva. He was a few years younger than my father and came from outside

Surany; he praised the yeshiva and said the town's Jewish community used to invite its young students for Shabbat meals, and he may have had meals at my grandparents' home. Subsequently I read that the yeshiva in Surany was well-known and attracted pupils from many countries, including Britain. Zvia got a kick out of me being in a yeshiva; her family kept kosher but was not religious. She used to send me letters, writing on the back of the envelope instead of sender details messages incompatible with the views of someone studying in a yeshiva. Zvia has beautiful handwriting and my father always complained that I didn't have handwriting like hers. There were also teachers who warned me that, because of my handwriting, I would not pass external exams such as the Bagrut, equivalent of A level, but I did. It was the early '60s and teenagers around the world worshiped the Beatles, Elvis Presley and others, but I listened to songs in Hebrew and only vaguely heard about rock 'n roll; I must have been fifteen or more when I heard of the Beatles and Elvis, but not about other international singers. I did not see what the craze was all about. There was one Israeli song that was forbidden to play in public: HaSelah HaAdom or the Red Rock, which referred to Petra in southern Jordan. In the '50s young Israelis would risk their lives crossing the border to visit Petra; many were killed, and the song was thought to encourage risky visits. My father liked only one singer, Shoshana Damari; she had a unique voice and I still like her songs.

At the beginning of my second year I left the yeshiva, not because of the food or missing girls; these were only at the background. During my study, I could not help my father in the farm, so in summer holidays between my first and second year I worked a lot on it to compensate. I sent my father, for the first time since arriving in Israel, for a week to his sister in Haifa. During that week my mother helped me, but I did most of the work. While in the yeshiva we used to have one weekend at home every three weeks; on the first such home visit in the second year, my mother told me that my father was not coping with the work and I should consider moving to the high school so I could live at home and help. I looked at my father, who obviously wanted me to study in the yeshiva, but he nodded in agreement with her. As far as I remember, this was the only time I was asked to help. That Saturday I spoke to my friends from the moshav, and Shimon Shifer said he also wanted to leave the yeshiva. Shimon had a twin brother, Aharon, who was not good at studying but was helping in the farm, so Shimon did not need to leave for the reason I did. I think already then Shimon was not really religious. Both Shimon and I walked over to Ein Tzurim to talk to Tova, who had been our teacher in the last two years of elementary school and now, as mentioned, was headmistress of the high school. We had some more talks and, in the end, I moved to the high school, but Shimon changed his mind and stayed in the yeshiva. Over the following months, more of my friends left the yeshiva, including Yitzhak Weisz and Israel Nedivi. We had to catch up in some subjects like chemistry, biology and physics. Generally speaking, high school was more fun than the yeshiva; the girls were not too happy with our re-joining them as they wanted to study, and we preferred to play. This came to a clash in the year before the last when one teacher lost his notes and blamed us, the boys – I don't remember all the ins and outs. The girls declared a boycott on the boys and did not speak to us for a few weeks. At some stage, in an attempt to make us study, Yitzhak and I were separated; I was made to sit near Rivka Amit and Yitzhak near Ester Feingenbaum. In that last year our class was small as those who did not expect to succeed in the Bagrut exams were asked to leave or left anyhow – too many failures would have been negative for the school.

Even after leaving, I felt connected to the yeshiva and often visited it, including during the traditional all-night studies of Shavuot, which was not practised in the moshav. When I went to university, Harav Druckman helped me secure a place in the dormitories and with a small student loan from the Mizrachi movement. Rabbi Druckman's wife was the local doctor in Shafir and some nearby settlements.

Today, as I have to accommodate my family members, I'm less strict than I was and would like to be. In a way religion today operates like a free marketplace: the options and choices are large, one is free to choose the level of observance and change it at any time. This is not exactly the case in the very orthodox communities where limited secular education, family pressure and financial dependency reduce the options. For me there is a beauty and value in religion and tradition that secular-only education misses.

FINAL SCHOOL EXAMS

I always had (and still have) difficulty in sitting for a long stretch; every so often I have to get up and move my legs. Perhaps it's a result of growing up in an open environment. Because I did not have a desk at home, I used to read and write by kneeling at the bed with the book or exercise book on it. This habit has stayed with me as I still use the bed in a similar way to do accounts, check bank statements etc.

As Bagrut exams got closer, I tried to study more. I did not study English at all and used the time freed to catch up on other subjects. One day, Tova saw me in the library during an English lesson. She asked me if I was not doing English and tried to persuade me to start learning it, but I just did not. In my last year at school, someone from Zrachia started once a week to screen a movie in the wooden hut near my home. I often gave in to temptation and went to watch; anyway, it was so close to my home that I could hear the music and dialogue quite plainly.

The first exam was Mathematics, and I felt I did not do badly. It did not help push me to study more. In Gemmarah I was sure I would get ten out of ten; the exam was oral, and my teacher presented me to the examiner as someone likely to answer all the questions correctly. The examiner asked me a tricky one which I did not answer totally correctly, and I got only nine. I was very upset. I knew all fifty pages we had to learn well, at least partly because I was helping others learn them. I passed all the exams except English, which I did not take. After the last exam, the class went to the beach in Ashkelon to celebrate. Then we all went our separate ways. Because I was the oldest, I was the first to go to the army, on 4 August 1965.

THE ARMY

I had no idea what would happen to me in the army; what would I do, where would I be, with whom, etc. We did not have, in the moshav, enough older boys with army experience to give examples, guide or advise us. On 4 August I had to get up very early, walk for about a mile to the bus stop, take the bus north to the junction called Kastina where I could catch a bus going south to Beersheba's central station; from there I had to take a local bus to the army joining point. I had to wait ages for each bus, and it was excruciatingly hot; no air-conditioning anywhere and my journey seemed to be endless, as later that day we had to travel on an army lorry back northward, passing not far from my home, to Tel Hashomer army base. While waiting in Kastina for the bus to Beersheba I saw a familiar face; we both knew each other by sight only. He was from the well-established moshav of Kfar Warburg to where, after Shabbat, we used to go to see movies. As mentioned, we did not mix with the children of that moshav but now at the bus stop, when we realised that we both were about to join the army, we instantly became friends. The army separated us after three days but nearly not, as I am about to explain.

My new friend asked me what I was going to do in the army, to which I said that I had no idea. Why, he said, didn't I join him in volunteering to Sayeret Matcal, an elite combat unit? I'd thought about volunteering but decided I could not do it to my parents, but now I was thrown back to the prospect and this time deep in turmoil about it, as it was crunch time. I remember being unable to decide. Working in the farm had made me fit, and it was expected from those growing up in a kibbutz or moshav to volunteer for elite units. After three agonising days, I said 'no' and separated from my friend. I then stayed in the Tel Hashomer camp for a few further days. It was very uncomfortable; about fifty of us slept in corrugated metal huts dating from the British Mandate. My uniform was too big, and the hat did not sit comfortably on my small head. I was not used to socks and shoes so at breaks, while everyone ran to the canteen to get refreshments, I just took off my boots and socks. One morning, I, or more accurately my personal number, was called to attend what we called shuk avadim, or slave market, because of the way personal numbers were called and everyone had to move to a particular point from where you were taken to the unit you were about to join. I was surprised to be told that I had volunteered to take part in training to be a pilot; unsure what to do, I went along, as only a few of those volunteering were accepted – the ones who were were ecstatic, as it was their dream. Like everyone else, during my last year in school, I had undergone various tests for the army; after the tests, I received a personal letter from the then commander of the air force, the legendary Ezer Weitzman, nephew of the first Israeli president and future president himself, saying that I had the necessary attributes – the slogan was 'hatovim letayiss', or 'the good ones to be pilots' – and asking me to volunteer. As an only child, I had to get my parents' confirmation, so I never replied. At the air force base, I had, for the first time since enlisting, food that I could eat – I could not eat the usual army food, having been spoilt by my mother. After more tests I was sent home to obtain my parents' approval, which I did with the help of a little lie. I told my worried parents that I would start the training but after a few months I would ask to end it; that way I would serve the rest of my military days in the relative comfort and safety of the air force. In truth, this was not my intention. At the base I met Zvi Havash, who'd grown up in our moshav and was a few months older than me; he'd trained and served as a technician. With his help I sat in a Mirage fighter, on the ground only of course. I'd never sat in a private car until I started to hitchhike during my military service, but it took some time as I was not familiar with the roads and location of towns, so I used buses mainly. It is strange that I sat in a Mirage fighter plane before ever sitting in a car. Zvi also took me to see a movie and in the air force the seating is based on rank so I, with no rank yet, sat in the front row just below the screen and perhaps strained my eyes.

The next day I failed some eye tests and was thrown out and back to Tel Hashomer, where I and a few others were called to an interview with the then chief military rabbi, HaRav Shlomo Goren. He wanted us to join his team, which I most definitely did not want to do. He described how he saw my future with fast track progress; I replied in some fear – after all, he had the rank of general – that I thought I was going to do something else. HaRav Goren was a stubborn person who did not give up easily, but after some more exchanges I was told to get out and, for the next few weeks, doing basic training, I plotted to ensure that I would do something else. Because of the number of youngsters, or baby boomers, my age, there was no room for all in the usual training base and a field base was created for some in the middle of nowhere. We spent the whole training period in tents. It was summer, hot, dusty and unpleasant. I hardly ate anything. At the end of basic training, I was called back to meet HaRav Goren in his office in Tel Aviv, where I remained for two days. I had two meetings with him, and he tried to convince me again to join his team. It was the first time that I saw something of Tel Aviv and the first time I slept a night there, not including when I was a sick toddler.

While I was hanging around the building where the military Rabanut was, I overheard the top ranks making negative comments about each other and secretly listening to each other's phone calls. Needless to say, this made me more determined not to join the military Rabanut. It reminded me of something my father had told me years before: when he was studying at the yeshiva, he was asked to accompany their rabbi to a spa town for a holiday; as it happened, another rabbi from another yeshiva was holidaying in the same spa and the two rabbis were very rude to each other; my father was shocked and, after that, did not automatically follow every rabbi's dictates. In the end, with help from my school, I did something easy: Madrich Gadna, or youth training (Gadna is Hebrew acronym of Gdudei Noar or youth battalions). This was ironic as I usually hadn't attended Gadna lessons in school and, when we had a whole day of Gadna activities, I'd stay at home to help on the farm. During my military service I did not like Rabbi Goren, but from a distance of fifty years I am full of admiration for what he achieved. He was brave both in the military sense and as a rabbi in the orthodox world. He helped converts; he released the widows of the sailors of the submarine *Dakar*, which disappeared in 1968, from being agunot, or chained women, long before finding the sunken submarine; most importantly, he created the Rabanut Hatzvait or military Rabanut. The military Rabanut ensured that the whole army had a Jewish identity; the original intention had been for orthodox soldiers to serve in separate units. HaRav Goren was appointed by Ben Gurion himself. His strong character ensured the success of a stately vision. He also believed that the Halacha, or Jewish law, had to take into account the reality of life in the modern era. He was a problem solver and issued many rulings and wrote books. But like many rabbis, he was too political.

In the Gadna, for the first time I met privileged youngsters who had money. Most of those involved in youth training were spoiled brats; a few had fathers who were high-ranking officers and managed to arrange comfortable close-to-home service for their children. As the base was near Tel Aviv, the families of many in the training course came to visit on Friday afternoons. Obviously my parents could not visit me. The journey from Shafir took hours as you had to go on the slow and only available bus, number 301, to Tel Aviv central bus station, then change to another slow bus going north. All the roads around the Tel Aviv central station were a disaster, especially on Friday and Sunday. I'd get off at Glilot, near where sixteen years earlier my parents and I had lived in a maabara, and walk for fifteen minutes to the camp. Sometimes I managed to hitchhike this last part of the journey. Once a week we had a one-to-one meeting with our direct commander, who commented that there was a difference between me and the others in the course. If a free evening or similar was cancelled, I would just turn around and get on with whatever I had to do as if I didn't care, while the others got into a state, crying and pleading. I explained that I definitely cared but I lived in a moshav where we were at the mercy of the elements and life was difficult and one had to carry on no matter how many setbacks one had. What I did not say was that the others were spoilt, and I was not.

I was given a day off a few times to help my father. I don't think the camp ever had many soldiers like me. To illustrate a difference, I'll mention the showers: when we came back to the base after being in the fields for a few days, everyone was desperate to wash but wanted to wait for the water to heat up (training took place during winter months), which took about two hours. I, on the other hand, remembering cold showers as a child, jumped in the shower immediately, which gave me an extra two hours' sleep. Even today I can have a cold shower in winter, and every morning I use cold water even if the water is freezing, as it can be in English winter. Also, because of work on the farm, I was very fit and found the training easy while the spoiled children were unfit and found it quite difficult. The only exciting part of the training was that sometimes we participated in maaravim, or ambush guarding, in groups of three or four near the border with Jordan at night. I also liked our masaot nivutim, or walks with the help of maps and the stars. In a group being trained parallel with us was someone called Chofni Cohen, who was very musical and entertained us. In 1978 his younger brother, Izhar Cohen, won the Eurovision song contest with his song A-BA-NI-Bi.

When I finished training, I was assigned to the southwest part of Israel as a Madrich Gadna; this area included my old school. To the surprise of some of my teachers, I was back with them, but this time in the teachers' room. I had an easy army service, moving among schools in the Ashkelon and Sderot area, and most nights I was able to sleep at home. This was fantastic and, most importantly, I was able to help my father on the farm. To save travelling time, I bought a scooter at the end of my first year; it enabled me to help even more on the farm but also to have some pleasurable activities like going to the beach in Ashkelon. I took my duties seriously and had a few tricks. For example, standing to one side before the pupils first met me, I picked up the names of a few calling and talking among themselves; when we were introduced, I would then address them by name, which usually impressed them. During military service I met many non-religious girls; some I really liked, but because I was religious and they not, I did not get involved beyond platonic relations. Once between assignments near Shafir, we had some free time and I brought one of the girls home with me. My mother was excited and prepared food while I showed my guest the farm. My mother then talked to her in broken Hebrew, and I could see that she was eyeing her as a possible daughter-in-law. Others in my unit had already pointed out that the girl liked me, but there never was anything between us. At the time, I thought she mainly liked to ride on my scooter. A few weeks after I'd bought it, I was driving well over the speed limit when suddenly I saw in the mirror a civilian policeman on a motorbike chasing me. I had to stop, and he said he was going to book me; as I was in uniform, it meant that I would be court-martialled – not a pleasant prospect. At that point one of my old school buses, upgraded from the original lorries, stopped nearby; it was empty after dropping off pupils. The driver knew me and knew the policeman; he assured the policeman that I would never do it again, and I was not booked. The roads in that part of Israel then were quite empty, and the temptation to speed was too strong. Much later, I was sitting next to the driver of a military vehicle; after returning pupils to their school, we were speeding when the driver saw in his mirror a police car some way behind. If caught, I would also be court-martialled as by then I was a sergeant-major responsible for the vehicle. I'm not going to say what exactly we did; I will only say that I knew the area well. Later that day, when I thought about the episode calmly, I regretted what we'd done, but it was too late to reverse it.

Youth training included Masaot, or trips when everyone slept in tents and walked quite a lot; some schoolteachers used to accompany us on these trips. During one, a married teacher from Ashkelon, not many years older than me, followed me around and tried to be close to me. I tried to lay down boundaries and keep a distance. After the trip there were rumours in the school that there had been something between us, so not only did she not succeed in what she wanted but others thought she had succeeded. We both denied that anything had happened, but I'm not sure how convincing we were; anyway, I was very innocent and naive. The highlight of the service was in summer, when sixteen-year olds from all over the country would gather for intensive six-week training and sporting activity. There were two training camps in the country: one in Glilot and the other, for religious pupils, at my old school. I was of course assigned to the religious one, so I was near home but could not sleep at home; in fact, I was hardly able to visit my parents for seven weeks as, in addition to the six week course, we had one week of preparation. I was in this training camp three times, and it was fun; the children behaved well – they had volunteered and given up most of their summer holiday for it, and it was amazing how in a few weeks their sporting abilities improved. I especially noticed this in gymnastics. My last such camp was just after the Six Day War when there was a huge demand from pupils for the camps; we then also had non-religious pupils, and they did not mind joining in the prayers, especially on Shabbat. In these camps there were also some religious soldier girls who chose to go into the army rather than use their exemption from service. Naturally there were close relationships, but never beyond the usual self-imposed boundaries. I was wondering whether any of the religious girls could become my future wife, but I was too young and anyway I was not sure, so I did not try pursuing anyone. I remember only two: one called Puah from moshav Beit Meir near Jerusalem and the other whose surname was Elmaliach. Some girls from my class also went into the army but to the Nachal, acronym for Noar Chalutzi Lochem or Pioneering Fighting Youth, which combined military service with farming. A few years ago, when living in Monaco, I met another Chaim; we compared notes and discovered that he had been a pupil in my last camp, and we both were in the same photo all those many years ago.

Sometime during army service Michael Shtekler, who did not like to study, had an accident on his motorbike. He was badly injured, and Shimon Friedman, also from Shafir, who was sitting behind him, was killed. Although Rafi and I were not close to Michael, we went to donate blood for him. Mati Yitzhaky, a friend from Or Etzion, was wounded during a routine army exercise – inadvertently he kicked a grenade that exploded – and I drove on my scooter from Shafir all the way to Rambam Hospital in Haifa and back the same day to visit him. One of the places I served in was the training place for the Mossad, or secret service; we saw them in civilian clothes and for some time did not know who they were. I did not take part in the mischievous games of some of my colleagues: they would phone civilian numbers pretending to be from the telephone company and inform the listener that the lines were being washed and cleaned, asking the poor person at the other end to bring a bucket; or they would send new arrivals to our unit to go to the kitchen and bring powdered electricity (the kitchen had a sufficient supply) or similar. In my experience army service was not a good example of the melting-pot – we had too many privileged soldiers – but my miluim service, or annual reserve service of about a month a year, definitely was.

Home before military service

WATER

Israel and the whole Middle East suffers from lack of water, and from an early age it was drummed into us not to waste water. The Bible describes how a canal (Kings II; 20, 20) was built to bring water to Jerusalem, and that canal still exists. From Roman times there are remains of viaducts. Theodor Herzl, father of modern political Zionism, also had, in the late 19th century, some ideas relating to moving water in the then Palestine. A British 1939 White Paper about the future of Palestine cited lack of water as one of the reasons to restrict Jewish emigration. In 1953 Israel started building Hamovil Haartzi, or the national carrier, to carry water southward from the Kineret, or Sea of Galilee. As children we combined school trips with visits to follow the progress of the project. One of the two main pipes of Hamovil Haartzi passes not far from Shafir. The project supplies both drinking water and water for irrigation. Water shortage forced Israel to be innovative, and reclamation of water is very advanced. I remember that in Nachal Lachish, there was a small structure, like a large screw, to capture river water and direct it into the ground to bolster the underground aquifer. An important innovation was the dripping of water direct into plants. There is the worldwide problem of desert expansion due to climate change and of mankind interfering with the balances of nature. Apparently, Israel is the only country where the desert is in retreat because of correct nature management. Today desalination of sea water and recycling of used water bridges the gap and provides enough water to allow for more to remain in the Kineret and to flow through the River Jordan into the Dead Sea. In some of the last few years, drought was so prolonged and severe that the national carrier was used to put water into the Kineret rather than pump water out. Every winter, newspapers report daily about the water level of the Kineret, and I follow it even from London. Water, or more accurately, lack of it, was a reason for the war I describe next.

THE SIX DAY WAR

During 1965 and '66 there was a mitun or recession in Israel and people had difficulty finding jobs; all that changed in 1967. A few months before the end of my service the Six Day War happened. I remember the three agonising weeks when everyone was waiting and it felt like the Arab countries were tightening a noose around us. In particular, I remember the prime minister Levy Eshkol, who was also defence minister, addressing the nation live on radio; he got stuck, stumbling over his words. Eshkol lacked confidence and charisma; the country was really under siege. Problems had started a few weeks earlier as the Syrians were working to divert sources of the River Jordan, which, as described, is vital to Israel for water. Israel sent fighter planes to bomb and stop the work. There were several 'dog fights', as jets from both countries engaged in mid-air combat. These fights resulted in a large number of Syrian planes being shot down, but no Israeli ones. Egypt, which still called itself The United Arab Republic (until 1971) although political union between Egypt and Syria had ended in 1961 (it was formed in '58), came to the defence of Syria. Initially it was rhetoric and no action, but in the Middle East, more than once, rhetoric ended in war. If you turned on the radio and moved the waves, 90% of what you heard was in Arabic and, even if you did not understand that language, you could feel the threat. One of the Arabic stations was in Hebrew; it was called Kol Haraam, from Cairo; kol is voice and Raam is thunder, but it was also the acronym in Hebrew of the United Arab Republic. Apart from hilarious mistakes in Hebrew, their broadcasts were really threatening.

Amid an escalating war of words, Nasser, Egypt's ruler ordered the UN to remove its peace forces stationed since 1956, as mentioned, on the border between Israel and Egypt. The UN rushed to do as Nasser said, and war felt closer and closer. Israel called up reservists, and soldiers' leaves were cancelled; the papers were full of pictures of soldiers and civilians digging trenches and filling sandbags. With so many reservists called up (lorries and vans were called also), the country came near to a standstill. Roads were full of military vehicles and equipment taken from emergency warehouses. Eshkol's disastrous radio broadcast, which sent a shiver down my spine, and probably most Israelis', was a turning point. Eshkol was forced to create a unity government with Menachem Begin, the eternal opposition leader, and Moshe Dayan, the military hero, as defence minister. Dayan said publicly that, with the surprise element lost, it would be difficult to wage a war; evidently, he was trying to mislead the Arabs into believing that a pre-emptive Israeli strike was not imminent.

Not being a combat soldier, I was assigned to help unload the expected wounded from helicopters at Ashkelon hospital. I remember on the morning of 5 June seeing from the hospital roof wave after wave of planes flying towards the sea; they flew very low and you could see the bombs they were carrying. It was a classic 'blitzkrieg', and the outcome was decided in the first three hours. Israel had launched a pre-emptive strike; all those heavily loaded planes bombed the Egyptian airfields, making them unusable. With the Egyptians grounded, the next stage was to destroy the planes themselves. The hour of attack was also a surprise, as the Egyptians had expected any attack to come at dawn, but this one was later, by which time their army had relaxed and was off guard. Also, the planes did not fly straight to Egypt but, as I saw myself, indirectly via the sea. Egyptian radio was broadcasting that their forces were advancing towards Tel Aviv. I saw families in Ashkelon, near the Gaza strip, rushing to the local bus station to evacuate to Tel Aviv, as they believed the broadcasts. In contrast, all Israeli radio said was that fighting had broken out on the border with Egypt and quoted what the Egyptian radio broadcast. No wonder some families in Ashkelon believed the Egyptians.

We were able to understand from wounded soldiers that the reality was different; in fact, the war had run away from us. After a few hours, there was only a trickle of helicopters, as Gaza had been conquered quickly and the wounded from fighting in the Sinai were taken to the Soroka hospital in Beersheba, nearer the battlefield. In the evening of the first day, Chaim Herzog, a retired head of Intelligence in the Israeli Army and later president of Israel, discussed the war on the radio. He quoted foreign sources as reporting that, not only were the Egyptians not progressing into Israel, but the opposite: the Israeli army was progressing into Sinai. Herzog's account of the war continued every day and was reassuring to everyone in Israel. One of those who believed the Egyptian lies was King Hussein of Jordan. Jordanian forces started firing on Tel Aviv from Kalkilia and also fired into the Israeli part of divided Jerusalem. Israel had not expected Jordan to join the war and had to divert forces from the south. Tanks and other military vehicles drove to Jerusalem rather than being transported in the usual way on specially-designed transporters, which were not available. The roads were damaged, but no one cared. Within the first four days Israel reached the Suez Canal and conquered the whole of the West bank. The fight in and around Jerusalem was fierce as the opponent was the Jordanian army, much better than the Egyptian or Syrian. An added dimension was the sensitivity associated with Jerusalem and its Holy places, which are special to so many around the world. Israel had relatively high casualties in Jerusalem as the unexpected fight against a better-fighting enemy was also against the clock, international political intervention being likely. On the fifth and sixth days of the war, Israel fought the Syrians and conquered the menacing Golan Heights. For many years, the Israelis living below the Heights had been subject to firing from Syrians above. Obviously it was difficult to fight climbing up a steep mountain and it was here that a friend, Dudi, was killed; he was the only friend of mine killed in this war. For nearly two thousand years Jews had not fought and now they were so good at it. I'm not praising this, just pointing out a strange fact.

In an unexplained incident, Israel shot down one of its own planes, killing the pilot; I think he was called Yoram Harpaz. He was flying towards the nuclear facilities in Dimona in the Negev and not responding to instructions to change course. There was also the bombing, on 8 June, by Israel of the United States technical research ship *Liberty*; thirty-four crew were killed and 171 wounded. The ship was in international waters close to Sinai. Israel apologised and paid compensation. Both Israel's and the US's investigation concluded that the incident was a mistake, but some people believe it was deliberate. One bomber from Iraq managed to reach Israel; it dropped bombs over Netanya, killing one woman and wounding a few people. It bombed a few other places before being shot down by an Israeli fighter. Unfortunately, it crashed onto an army base, killing sixteen reservists; it could have caused much greater damage.

When we heard that Jerusalem, including the Kotel and Temple Mount, was taken, and soon the whole of the West Bank up to the River Jordan under Israeli control, we were ecstatic. In an incredible coincidence, Naomi Shemer had composed the song 'Yerushalayim Shel Zahav', or 'Jerusalem of Gold', just a few weeks before to compete for Israel in the Eurovision Song Contest. It failed to win, but it became the song of our victory; the original included words lamenting that one could not visit parts of Jerusalem. After the war Naomi Shemer adjusted them, as now everyone was able to go to the holy places. Even today when I hear the song, it brings tears to my eyes and memories of these historical days return.

From the second day of the war we had nothing to do, so a group of us took an army lorry and drove into Sinai; seeing so many dead Egyptian solders affected me. A few weeks later I went again into Sinai on an organised trip of my unit, all the way to the Suez Canal. I have a photo of myself by the canal. The scars of war were still evident and, as I explained to my elder son, who asked me years later why unlike most Israelis we never travelled to Sinai, I did not want to go there again. Going just after the war's end first to the Kotel, then the old city of Jerusalem, and later to other cities that until then had been under Jordanian rule, had for a short time an effect on me of believing that we lived in Messianic times and the next thing would be the appearance of the Messiah. I think everyone going to Jerusalem went first to the Kotel and not the Temple Mount, as for two thousand years of exile the Kotel, also known as the Wailing Wall, symbolised the tragedy of the Jewish people and our yearning to be able touch something from the past. For many Jews, the stones of the Kotel have a human heart.

During the coming months, one freely moved about in the Gaza strip and the West Bank; I even went to have a haircut in Gaza, as it was cheap. We also bought Pepsi, which we could not get in Israel because Pepsi had given in to the Arab boycott. On a trip with my parents and others, we drove through an Arab village, and my mother said: 'Do you see the hate in the eyes of the Arabs when they see us?' I was brought down to earth at once; obviously in the euphoria of victory, I saw nothing, but my mother, who had seen hate in Europe, noticed it instantly. My growing up in Israel meant that I was insulated from many of the phenomena that had affected my parents. From then on, I thought we should live separately from the Arabs in the West Bank, or as it was known again Yehuda ve Shomron, or Judea and Samaria. That does not mean I don't feel connected to the holy places and ancient land where our forefathers lived, but we have to live in the real world. In the same way that we travelled freely to Gaza and the West Bank, the Arabs from there travelled freely into Israel. The road near Shafir was full of Arab cars; there was active trade between Israelis and Arabs, and many Arabs found work in Israel. I particularly recall us selling manure to Arabs, as the Gaza strip was desperate to fertilise the soil. When we would fertilise with manure, a tractor was used. An exception was with the best manure, which was produced by chickens: we had to clear it with shovels and wearing wellies, as no tractor was able to enter the cages where chickens were kept. The Arabs did not use tractors, only shovels, and were barefoot; as payment was per lorry, they used to step, barefoot, on the manure in the lorry to make room for more. Most Israeli girls and women, like in the rest of the world, did not cover themselves from top to toe, and many Arabs found that confusing, for lack of a better word, especially miniskirts. A few of them would pinch the exposed skin of the Israeli women.

Over the next few years most of my friends established settlements in the West Bank. The land was cheap, and one was able to build a beautiful house for the cost of a simple flat in towns around Tel Aviv. Gush Emunim, or Bloc of the Faithful, was established in the home of Rabbi Drukman, who still lives in the community centre near my school, now called Merkaz Shapira, or Shapira Centre. Gush Emunim is at the forefront of establishing new settlements in the West Bank. There is a geographical dimension to religious studies, and Gush Emunim consisted mainly of religious people, but non-religious people also supported the settlement movement. With so much new territory and military commitment, military service was extended first from two years and four months to two and half years, then to three years. I travelled a lot over Gaza, the West Bank and the Golan Heights and regularly visited the holy places. A few weeks after the war when the 'no man' areas along the border in the heart of Jerusalem were cleaned from mines and bombs and the border between the Israeli and Jordanian parts of Jerusalem opened up, I made a trip that was special for me. I went the whole length of the pre-1967 divide and absorbed the new reality. I remembered that we used to go to certain parts of the border like the derelict Notre Dame, Mandelbaum Gate, Mount Zion and kibbutz Ramat Rachel, close to the tomb of Rachel, which had been under Jordanian rule and how we used to look at the enemy and life on the other side. We were able to see the tops of the Al Aksa and Omar Mosques and busy life in the Arab part of Jerusalem. Mandelbaum Gate was famous, as it was the official crossing point between the two parts of the city. I went everywhere in Jerusalem except the Temple Mount: we were advised by religious authorities not to go there so that we didn't, inadvertently, walk into the part where the Holy of Holies used to be. (The precise location was assumed but uncertain.) This ruling resulted in *de facto* abandonment of Temple Mount to the Moslems; however, nowadays many religious people do go there. One of the few rabbis who thought it was permitted was HaRav Goren; he even established a small post of the military Rabanut on the Temple Mount, which Dayan ordered to be removed. Another special trip was from the Dead Sea to the Judaean mountains all the way up to Hebron; this trip came during Chanukah in the winter of 1967. We had beautiful weather and the scenery was incredible. I remember one of my colleagues from the Gadna falling in love with one of the border police who helped in guarding us; their relationship went on at least until I finished army service in August 1968, though they were from very different backgrounds.

A group of us arranged walks a few months before the end of our military service, by which time the girls from our class who'd gone into the Army would be discharged, as they served only two years. We were all from Massuot, Shafir and Merkaz Shapira. I remember Israel Nedivi, Rivka Amit and Ester Feingenbaum. We walked to nearby Kibbutz Negba, famous for its stand against the Egyptian army in The War of Independence, and other local areas. Ester and I also took a trip, the two of us on my scooter, to the Galil and Ramat Hagolan or the Golan Heights. I have no recollection of how this idea came up, but it was a great trip. We stayed first night at my aunt and uncle's in Haifa; they were totally smitten by Ester, especially my aunt who spoke to Ester in Hungarian. We then continued through the Galil, staying for

Shabbat at a youth hostel in Tsfat with meals booked at a kosher hotel. At the hotel we met another Ester and her husband, Moshe, who were on their honeymoon. This Ester knew the artist who was my mother's friend from Czechoslovakia and whose doctor sister had stopped me having my tonsils out twenty years earlier; later she and Moshe lived near me in Ramat Gan. From there we drove through the Golan Heights. As appropriate in those days for religious people, we did not touch each other. There was only one embarrassing moment: when we were registering in a youth hostel (separate rooms for males and females), we were asked by the receptionist if we were chaverim or friends, a Hebrew term in those days used also to indicate that a boy and a girl were a couple. We both turned red and were silent until one of us realised that the receptionist was asking if we were members, the Hebrew word for which is also chaverim; if we had answered yes, we would have been entitled to a discount. Because my military service was extended twice, altogether to three years, on the day of my discharge I received a cheque for nearly a thousand lirot. As neither I nor my parents had a bank account, I stopped in the town called Yavneh, which was on my road home, to find a post office so I could take the pay in cash. On my arrival home I gave it all to my parents.

UNIVERSITY

During my service I came across people from different sections of Israeli society and, as mentioned before, especially the better off sections. I wanted to advance and started to read books in English, simple ones at first, then gradually more difficult ones. I still felt trapped in the moshav and thought I had no chance to make it in a big city, so I decided to study agriculture, which was taught partly in Jerusalem and partly in Rehovot, to which it was possible to commute in one bus ride from Shafir. I went to the university and collected the registration forms but, before handing them back, the war broke out. During my added military service I changed my plan of studying at the Hebrew University to studying economics at Bar Ilan University in Ramat Gan. I think victory in war made us more optimistic in general; also, I thought, there would be more opportunity with the enlarged territory and population. Two of my friends, Rafi Shlesinger and Zvi Itzkovitch, planned to study economics at Bar Ilan; as mentioned, I received a little help in financing my tuition and residence in the dormitories. Avraham Levinger from Shafir also came to study economics with us, but he was part time and did not live in the dorms.

Rafi and I shared a small room with an American chap. Both of us chose to study Extended Economics, so we did not have a minor subject. We did have to study Jewish subjects, a requirement of Bar Ilan, which was a religious university with non-religious students who, on arrival, put on a kipa and, on leaving, took it off. The Economics department was like a factory. Some two hundred students started the course, sitting in crowded rooms. It was difficult and demanding; luckily Rafi was more disciplined than I, so he forced me to study. At the start, I never opened my mouth in the lessons as there were students from well-known and posh schools, and I thought they must be much cleverer. This changed after the results of our first exams were published. I got good marks, above those of students from the posh schools. This gave me some confidence, but I continued to have doubts. Because our school had not been able to teach us high level mathematics, Rafi and I and others had to catch up. It was very hard and, just when the first maths exam was due, I had to go to miluim and take the exam in moed beit, or the second date, with those who had failed first time or, like me, missed the first sitting. I just got a pass, which gave me no boost. In the second year there was an important exam that I missed because of miluim and again had to take moed beit. I was not aware that some of my fellow students had an elaborate plan to smuggle the exam to someone outside, known as very clever, to answer the questions. The answers were smuggled back in, and a number of students copied them; I was offered the answers but declined – as said, I did not cheat. What happened was that I got most of the answers right, unlike the answers that were smuggled in. Nearly everyone failed and the university did something – I think it was called 'factoring' – and everyone's result was upgraded, so I got a very good mark. I doubt if even half of those who started graduated.

During our studies Rafi and I continued helping in the farm. We arranged our timetable so that on Sundays and Tuesdays we started courses in the afternoon and had no lessons on Fridays. On Fridays we travelled on my scooter at about five in the morning and worked all day in the farm. Every Shabbat we were with our parents, and on Sundays we worked again in the farm most of the day, returning to the university in the late afternoon. On Tuesdays, again we left the university very early for Shafir, working all day and back to the university late afternoon. With work and study, we had no free time. To save time I stopped shaving and started to grow a beard. We ate in the university dining room. To save money we ate a lot of bread, which was cheap; and we met up with other pupils we knew from the past like Rivka Amit or new friends. Anyone who did not know English well had to take a yearlong course; there were three levels. Rafi and I were placed in the middle level and our friend from Shafir, Mordi, who studied criminology, was in a different class. Our teacher was one Emma Solomon; she looked very young and was clearly extremely clever; coincidently she was also Mordi's teacher. We sometimes ate with her in the dining room – she often used the student section, not the lecturers' section.

In this period after the Six Day War Israelis were able to travel in an area three times as big as before. But for Rafi and me, studying and working took most of our time. We did meet some girls but only superficially, and we certainly did not travel anywhere. We went to one or two gatherings to hear Uri Zvi Greenberg, the right-wing firebrand poet. We followed the news a little and knew that Charles de Gaulle, the French president, had imposed an embargo on Israel, even refusing to deliver planes and boats that had been paid for. De Gaulle had decided to switch sides and support the Arabs. It was obvious what had prompted this: for years France had fought the Arabs in North Africa, but after much bloodshed its former colonies gained independence so it was keen to mend relations with the Arab world and dumped Israel. The effect was serious as until then only France had sold weapons to Israel. There were demonstrations against De Gaulle; Rafi and I joined one in December '68. We heard speeches at what was then called Kikar Malchei Israel, or the Kings of Israel Square, later renamed after Yitzhak Rabin. After the speeches, we marched toward the French Embassy in Hayarkon Street near the sea. En route we bumped into our English teacher, Emma, who was also demonstrating. You may remember that I did not study English at school and did not take the English Bagrut or final exam. I was accepted to university on condition that I pass an English exam within the first year. Rafi out of the blue asked Emma if she would agree to give me private English lessons.

A side point: for the next fifty years Israel was dependent on the USA for weapons, not in the same way that she had been on France but dependent still. The difference now is that Israel itself has become one of the biggest exporters of weapons, and its military industry is very advanced.

As mentioned, there had been some contact between Emma and me outside the classroom, and I noticed she was seeking my company. I also wanted to be in her company. Sometimes I would daydream about her, but it seemed unrealistic. Anyway, with the indirect help of the French president and the direct help of Rafi, we arranged that I come to Emma for English private lessons. As it happened, she lived in Tel Aviv in Nordau Boulevard, which was one of the few streets I knew in that city. This totally shy and inexperienced youngster came to learn English, but Emma from Hampstead, an upmarket area of London, was more experienced in life and the English lessons were soon forgotten. I don't remember exactly who said what, but we were clearly very attracted to each other. Later, Emma told me that she was attracted to me because I had blue eyes. I don't think I had noticed, until Emma told me, that I had blue eyes; anyway, I don't care about colours. I did not speak much English and Emma did not speak much Hebrew, but we managed. On my next trip to my parents, I told them I had found the girl I wanted to marry. The difference between my background and Emma's was big, in every aspect. She came from a large Sephardi family and lived in a nice, big house in a nice part of a large and important city; I came from a small Ashkenazi family living in a dilapidated house in a rural area in the middle of nowhere. Her father had been a high-ranking civil servant and also a successful writer and had even stood, unsuccessfully, as a candidate for the British parliament; we, in contrast, worked as farmers, standing every day deep in manure. Emma was Reform, I was Orthodox; Emma was working, I was a penniless student with debt. I'm punctual, Emma is not; I'm flexible, Emma is not. I eat to live, Emma lives to eat. I could go on, but it will be simpler to say that I can't think of anything that is same between us.

One Friday a few weeks later, Emma came with me to Shafir for Shabbat. Rafi was in the loop as to what was going on but not Mordi; we did not see him much as he combined extended military service with studying. In synagogue that Friday evening I asked Mordi to pop round to me after dinner; Rafi was coming as well. When Mordi saw Emma at our home he was speechless and surprised as, clearly, she must be staying locally because of Shabbat; but where? He asked Emma: 'Are you staying in kibbutz Ein Tzurim?' We told him what was going on. We decided to get married in Tel Aviv on the 27 March 1969 in a synagogue called Ichud Shivat Zion or United Return to Zion in Ben Yehuda Street (the old building on the west side of the street). The name of the synagogue is an irony; not only did Emma eventually not return to Zion, but she forced me also to leave. Another minor irony, similar to me being a madrich Gadna, was that I did not attend English classes at school and now I was marrying an English teacher. As far as Jewishness, Emma's family were very Zionist. I met Emma's sister, Celia, who while at Oxford University had become orthodox and, like Emma, came to Israel after the Six Day War, which had affected not only Israelis but Jews all over the world. There was a difference between the two sisters: Celia had from much earlier on wanted to live in Israel. With Emma's parents and family in London, Emma and I had to make the wedding arrangements. Every Friday we went to my parents for Shabbat on my scooter. Rafi's mother asked me to drive very carefully as, she told me, engaged couples are in greater risk than others. My parents, especially my mother, embraced Emma totally, but Emma felt uncomfortable in Shafir; she felt that everyone looked at and examined her. On top of that, my parents and I conversed in Hungarian, the 'official' language of Shafir, and she felt excluded. Also, the physical conditions in Shafir were not great, although better than in the past and she had my room, while I slept on the veranda. Emma was especially sensitive to cold and the only heater we had was paraffin-based, which she could not take.

I found the following by chance a few months ago; it is a translation from German by Emma's father of the letter my mother wrote on 20 February 1969 to Emma's parents in reply to Emma's father's letter to my parents:

Dear Mr and Mrs Solomon,

I shall immediately answer your kind letter as time is already short and we shall soon (God willing) be getting to know one another personally.

We have taken at once to your dear Emma. Both girls are really very lovable (sympathique)! Chaim is our only child – and I am delighted to be getting such a precious daughter in Emma, and also that our Chaim is so happy (fortunate). I believe that this might be a lucky turn of fate, with Emma, we hope, making up to us for everything.

We look forward to the pleasure of seeing you soon and remain with cordial greetings to you and your dear wife.

Josef and Anna Klein

Motto

Emma did as Schiller said:

Then let him first who would be forever bound
Test if the right heart for his heart he's found

Unfortunately, I do not have the letter from Emma's father to my parents; I do remember that Emma wrote to her parents that it seemed that my parents' past had no resemblance to their present life in the moshav.

As time went by, more people in the university heard about us but we tried to keep our plans to ourselves. One of those in our class, Naomi Ilberg, was a mature student living not far from Emma, and Emma told her she was engaged to someone from the class and asked Naomi to guess whom. Naomi went through a few names before mine, which indicated that we were behaving correctly. Emma and my mother decided I had to wear a suit and tie for the wedding, and it was arranged that I meet the two of them in a well-known men's shop in Tel Aviv. This kind of thing was not on my mind (little changed in the next fifty plus years) and I arrived at the shop wearing sandals and a short-sleeved shirt. My mother was upset with me, and a stupid suit and even more stupid tie was chosen. I don't remember being bothered with practical details of the wedding – I did not attach much importance to where it would be, what would be served, etc. We had chosen Ichud Shivat Zion Synagogue as the venue and its rabbi to conduct the service; we were lucky that it was Rabbi Ansbacher, who spoke good English. With other couples we met him before the wedding, and I did not mind that it would not be conducted by the newish Rabbi of Shafir. Rabbi Ansbacher was a generous person and invited the Rabbi of Shafir to take part. Emma's parents arrived in advance of the event, and Emma's father made the rest of the arrangements. I hired a car (the first time I drove after learning to drive) and took them to meet my parents. As Emma's father spoke German, he and both my parents were able to communicate. Emma's mother was left out but, unlike Emma, was not bother by it.

Emma's parents were to pay all the costs of the wedding and even a few days honeymoon for us in Eilat. Britain in those days had strict currency controls and Emma's father had to keep all the invoices and receipts. When we were clearing Emma's parents' house after her mother's death, I found them. I will not bore you with all the costs, just two: the flowers cost 425 Israeli Lira and the cake 145. Emma was also to receive some money towards a flat. Unknown to me, Emma's father had approached my father and asked him also to contribute; my father, of course, agreed immediately but it was not easy for him to raise the money. We decided to buy a flat in Ramat Gan close to the university and saw a few flats in various stages of development. The biggest within our budget was on the third and last floor (without a lift) at number 22 Hayarden Street. The road was relatively wide, so I was afraid of noise, but it was not a through road, and it seemed to have little traffic. We bought the flat, which was due to be completed in four or five months. The money Emma was getting was in a trust; I had no idea what that meant but learnt quickly that this arrangement was not suitable in Israel. We had to have lawyers in England and Israel; the one in Israel, Giladi, was very nice and eventually found a practical solution by registering the trustees as having an interest in the flat; this meant that we could not get a mortgage. It would have been beneficial to have had a mortgage, as because of the high inflation the purchase power of monthly repayments was going down and down. By the time Celia got married Emma's father did not use a trust. The widow and children of the most famous Israeli spy, Eli Cohen, lived not far from our flat.

with Emma in Nazareth

WEDDING AND AFTER

The wedding was chaotic. In Israel in those days invitees did not confirm if they would come or not, and some guests brought friends. Also, some guests went at the food immediately, even before the Chupa or ceremony. It seems that our persecuted history makes us Jews too attached to food. I arrived by bus and not scooter direct from university with the tie in my pocket, and Tibi put it on for me. Emma's five aunts and one uncle had arrived specially from London; her brother did not come, nor the uncle living in Seattle. On my side, Zvia did not come as she had given birth shortly before. Many of my friends came, and the photos look nice. After a short honeymoon, we returned to the usual routine. We also went to a household goods shop and swapped duplicated presents – in some instances we had received five of the same – to items we needed. I gave up my residence at the university and we rented a room at someone's flat in 25

Dov Hoz street in the heart of Tel Aviv, where we lived uncomfortably for three and half months.

Emma had some Arab students and one of them, Hasan Azam, invited us to stay with his family in Nazareth over a weekend; a close friend of his was getting married. Because Hasan was best man, part of the ceremony was to take place in his house. On the relevant Friday Emma, Celia and I travelled by buses (three) from Tel Aviv to Nazareth. The arrangement was that Hasan would meet us at the central station. Typically, we arrived late, and Hasan had left, having given up on us. We did not have his address so asked if anyone knew Hasan. I was wearing a kipa as usual, and we were clearly three Jews while everyone, hundreds, around us were Arabs. At the end, a taxi driver heard us and said he was a cousin of Hasan and could take us to his house. This was 1969, but in later years I would not have dreamt of doing anything like it, and I'm sure Hasan would not have invited us – even if he had wanted to, he would have been afraid of his neighbours' reaction. We got into the taxi and the driver took us to the house of Hasan high up in the town, with beautiful views. Hasan's father had worked in a senior position in Nazareth town hall but had died a few years earlier. We were guests of honour and found a lot of similarities between Jewish and Muslim weddings. Our only discomfort was that Hasan's mother thought it inappropriate to have a toilet in the house, so similar to what we'd had in Shafir, but for a different reason, there was a hut at the end of the garden. It was a great weekend. We left after Shabbat and took buses back to Tel Aviv armed with a big box of Baklawa, which was our main food for the week. I do hope that such encounters will be possible again.

At the end of the academic year, we flew to London via Paris where we met my great uncle and two of my mother's cousins. It was the first time I'd flown out of Israel, and I don't recall being excited about Paris' or London's tourist sites; however, I was impressed by the yogurts in France as they had real fruit pieces in them, something we did not yet have in Israel. I was overwhelmed by the size of Emma's family; every day (nearly), I was introduced to new relatives. One of the first things Emma's father did was to take me next door to introduce me, his Israeli son-in-law, to Mrs Berlin, mother of the philosopher Sir Isaiah Berlin. When she died in her nineties a few years later, many of her books were put outside for passers-by to take; I took a few about Zionism and Palestine. Some years after, we met Sir Isaiah himself through his stepson, the publisher Peter Halban.

As Emma was a new immigrant to Israel, we were able to buy foreign goods without tax; so we borrowed money from Emma's father to purchase a car, furniture, kitchen equipment and a television, which we gave to my parents. Exchange rates in those days were fixed, and before I was able to repay the loan there was a devaluation in the Israeli Lira, and our debt to Emma's father went up dramatically. Emma was earning a salary, but I was still a student, in the second year, and had stopped going to Shafir to help my father. My father as a result could not continue to keep the farm and sold everything. He was sixty-six and said he had worked hard all his life and was allowed to stop; he occupied himself by growing vegetables, melons and watermelons etc. For years he had not wanted to apply for compensation from Germany for his suffering and losses in the Holocaust; I think it was too difficult for him to go through the process, reliving horrible times. My uncle began to work on him to change his mind, so finally he did apply and got a lump sum and monthly amount. My mother had applied earlier but due to technicalities had got nothing;

after what she'd gone through, this seemed very unfair. In the '50s there had been a big debate in Israel about whether to accept compensation from Germany. Menachem Begin led demonstrations against it, but the then prime minister, Ben Gurion, with the support of the Knesset had accepted. In Hebrew the compensation agreement was called 'heskem shilumim', or 'payment agreement', as no amount of money could compensate for what the Nazis had done.

Receipt of money made a big difference to my parents; they even opened a bank account. Around this time, the old houses in Shafir were deemed unsafe and to be demolished; some members had already moved out of them. New houses had been built by the prefabricated method, which not everyone liked as it was difficult to make changes and even hammering a nail into the wall was complicated. The mortgage terms were attractive but not the houses, and my parents with many others had not joined in the scheme. My father said that as long as he was alive, the old house would be suitable, but he had no option when the old house was scheduled to be demolished. The new houses now on offer were better than the earlier prefabs; my parents chose tiles that differed from the standard and made other improvements, which helped them enjoy the process. The payments from Germany came in handy, but sadly my father would never enjoy living in the new house because he died just as it was nearing completion.

Emma and I plus Celia would often spend Shabbat in Shafir; Celia also stayed with us on Shabbat when we were in Ramat Gan. We moved into our flat straight on return from London, 8 September 1969. The flat was not completely finished, and our furniture had not yet arrived, so we slept on mattresses on the floor. Emma's cousin Mallory and his wife Beatrice, who'd married the day before we left London, stayed with us as part of their honeymoon, also sleeping on mattresses. Over the years other relatives of Emma's came to stay. One was Johnny Palmer, who'd studied economics at Cambridge at the same time as I'd studied at Bar Ilan. I compared what we'd had to do with what he had and there seemed a big difference: we had many more courses and they were more mathematically-based. Another visitor who stayed was a cousin of Emma's parents from Australia, a professor of something and very absent-minded. He changed my view about punctuality: he wanted to buy his sister four silver kiddush cups for blessing over wine and went to a silver shop in Ben Yehuda Street in Tel Aviv but did not have enough money so arranged to return the next day. The next day, as usual, he was wasting his time and it was late afternoon before he left Ramat Gan for Tel Aviv. At five minutes to seven – shops close at seven – he got off the bus way before Ben Yehuda Street and totally by chance directly opposite a silver shop; here the cost of the same silver cups were half compared to the shop in Ben Yehuda Street so he bought eight cups and gave us four, which we still use every Shabbat. One thing that was very difficult for Emma was that we had to wait more than a year for a telephone, so each time we wanted to make a call we had to go to the nearest public phone. To use the public telephone, one needed an asimon or special token that one had to buy, but it was difficult to find them in shops as their cost kept going up and people hoarded them.

We did not have much in common with our neighbours, but on the ground floor lived the Nachmans, an older couple who had recently emigrated from Argentina. Mrs Nachman was nosey and observed everything happening in the house, so she noticed Celia and one day she told Emma that she had a nice sister and that she – Mrs Nachman, that is – had the Shiduch or match for her. Celia and Julio were introduced to each other in our flat and found that they both liked Menachem Begin; this was in 1970, seven years before Begin became prime minister.

In the third year of my studies, I took a full-time job in the economics department of the export division of Agrexco, Israel's government-owned agricultural export company. I cut some of my courses and on Tuesdays arrived at work at about eleven and stayed late. Office work was a new experience for me. I had to sit at a desk all day in a crowded room; there was plenty of gossip, intrigue and backstabbing. I liked most of the individuals I worked with but not the senior personnel. I had always been afraid that it would be difficult for me, without personal contacts, to find a job, but it turned out to be easy and, ironically, my agricultural background was an advantage. I used this work experience to write my final dissertation and got full marks. The dissertation was a detailed comparison of different methods of exporting agricultural goods, and Agrexco would shortly use it to improve transportation and save costs.

Celia and Julio got married in August 1970 in Kfar Hamaccabiah, near where we were living, and bought a flat also in Hayarden Street from the same contractor we'd used. This was helpful for Emma, who felt that social groupings in Israel were formed during school and army service and not open to new entrants, especially immigrants. She did not feel at home in my social network, and in Shafir people ignored her and Celia as if saying 'you are not welcome because you took one of our lads from us'. There were some exceptions such as Rivka, a mature student at Bar Ilan who lived not far from us. Rivka, who was pretty, practical and spoke five or more languages, had noticed Emma at university and saw that she was out of place and kind of adopted her. She became close to Emma's parents and aunts and 'part of the family', often staying with Emma's parents in London.

MILCHEMET HAHATSHAH OR WAR OF ATTRITION

The pre-1967 borders between Israel and its Arab neighbours had disappeared, but the new borders were not peaceful. There were sporadic clashes and both sides suffered casualties. Arab countries met on 29 August 1967 in Khartoum to declare the famous three No's: no peace with Israel, no recognition of Israel and no negotiations with Israel. Israel's prime minister was now Golda Meir; the defence minister was still Moshe Dayan. The period from March 1968 to August 1970 turned into what became later known as the War of Attrition, with Egyptian artillery shelling and commando raids resulting in an Israeli response. Israel found itself in a static war, something it was not used to; it built a fortress line along the Suez Canal, known as the Bar Lev line, named after the then Chief of Staff. As casualties on the Israeli side grew, Israel decided to use the air force to attack deep inside Egypt to deter the Egyptians from attacking our troops. Instead of stopping the attacks, this caused Egypt to ask the Soviet Union for help. During February and March 1970, thousands of Soviets soldiers arrived secretly in Egypt; in April scores of Mig 21s, the newest fighter planes also arrived with Soviet pilots, who were known not to think much of Arab pilots. Not wanting to fight the Soviets, Israel stopped its attacks deep into Egypt and operated only near the Suez Canal.

The USA, mediating between Israel and Egypt, restricted its sale of weapons to Israel; some say that this was because the USA wanted to be an honest broker while others say the

USA wanted to pressurise Israel into accepting ceasefire terms. As already mentioned, France had imposed an embargo on Israel. The Soviet pilots started to chase Israeli planes; then on 25 June they began trying to shoot down the planes, flying into Sinai and damaging one Israeli aircraft. Three days later the Soviet pilots again initiated a dog fight, again entering Sinai. With deterrence eroded, Israel decided to take the initiative and on 30 July operation 'Rimon 20' or 'pomegranate 20' took place. This was a sophisticated ambush. What Egyptian and Soviet radar operators saw looked like a usual Israeli Skyhawk plane flying from Sinai into Egypt to attack, followed by two reconnaissance planes to take photos to assess damage. Suddenly the reconnaissance planes turned out to be four, flying so close to each other that they had looked like two. Also, what looked like Skyhawks turned out to be the more powerful Phantoms; in addition, four Mirage planes appeared from nowhere. On top of it all, Israeli military intelligence, having intercepted the Soviets' communications lines, blocked them; and within six minutes fourteen Israeli fighter planes had downed five out of twenty-four Soviet planes, killing four Soviets pilots while suffering no casualties. Apparently, the Egyptians were happy that the Soviet pilots had been beaten by Israel. Eight days later, a ceasefire was arranged by the US, and the War of Attrition ended. Not everyone in Israel was happy with the ceasefire conditions, and Menachem Begin's party left the coalition government. A couple of months later, on 28 September (my father's birthday), Egypt's ruler, Nasser, died suddenly from a heart attack; Anwar Sadat replaced him and in 1972 expelled twenty thousand Soviet 'advisors'. The War of Attrition is a forgotten war: Israel suffered hundreds of soldiers' deaths, but while it was going on life in Israel continued as normal.

As the writer Chaim Guri wrote: 'Ha teala boeret ve Tel Aviv mueret' or 'the canal is burning and Tel Aviv is lit up'.

As mentioned, France had refused to deliver planes paid for by Israel. These were fifty Mirage 5s adapted to Israeli specifications. Israel responded by building an unlicensed copy of the plane (rumour was that Israeli spies obtained the technical specifications), calling it Nesher or Eagle; it entered into service in 1971. Israel started to develop a more capable plane, also based on the Mirage, called Kfir or lion cub, which entered service in 1975 and wasn't withdrawn until 1995, by which time the USA was selling Israel superior planes. Israel sold Kfir planes to a few countries and even the US Navy had leased twenty-five. Building the plane helped Israel create a meaningful aviation industry. The chief executive of Israel Aerospace Industries at the time was husband of a colleague of Emma's, teaching at Bar Ilan.

GRADUATION AND MY SECOND JOB

When I graduated, I did not go to the ceremony as I did not see the point. Based on the fact that I had graduated, I got immediately promoted at Agrexco, but I decided to look for a new and more challenging job. Again, it was easy: I went to work at Dun & Bradstreet, the American information company. This was more to my liking as I did not have to sit for long hours at a desk but got to travel and meet businesspeople. The company was small in Israel but carried on in-depth analysis of the economy, and I liked the personnel. When I told my father what I had done, he was alarmed: why had I left a government-owned company and moved to an American company that might leave Israel at any time whereas the previous job would have been for life?

What in fact happened twenty years later was that Agrexco was privatised and went bankrupt.

I was excited about my new job and spent a lot of time at it, both meeting people and writing reports. Most of the reports had to be in English; Emma helped me and greatly improved my skill. I did not follow the Olympics in Munich in the summer of 1972 as we did not have television and the Israeli athletes were not good enough to gain medals. This changed when Palestinian terrorists took eleven Israeli athletes hostage. Apparently, security arrangements at the Olympic village were deliberately light to look different from the Nazi-era Olympics of 1936. Emma's parents were with us, and we listened to the radio non-stop; late at night it was reported that the Germans had rescued the Israelis and killed the terrorists, and we went to sleep relieved. But when we got up, we heard that all eleven Israelis had been killed. Among them was Andre Spitzer, whose daughter, Anuk, was only a couple of weeks old. Years later when we dealt with Kfar Hamaccabiah, Anuk Spitzer was the person we were in contact with. Our future daughter-in-law, Alix, realised this and made the connection.

During one of my father's uncle Arnold's trips to Israel, we invited him for dinner at our flat; it must have been 1971. It was totally different from his visit to Shafir in the early '50s. Arnold came with his then girlfriend; Celia, and Julio came too, as well as the cultural attaché of the French embassy, a young woman who was doing research at the Hebrew University similar to what Emma was doing. Six languages were spoken around the table that evening: English, Hebrew, German, French, Spanish and Hungarian.

CHILDREN

Both Emma and I were now working, and we decided to start a family. Ariel was born on Friday afternoon 18 February 1972 in Tel Hashomer hospital. I took Emma to the hospital, a few minutes' drive from us, and was told there was no point in waiting as the birth was not going to happen quickly. In those days, husbands could not be present at the birth as there were a number of women giving birth in the same room at the same time. I anyway would have not wanted to attend as I remembered cows giving birth and did not like it; sorry, everyone. I returned home, went to sleep and when I woke up, I phoned a number given to me by the hospital and was told that Emma had already given birth, to a healthy boy. I told Emma's parents, who were staying with us, and left a message for my parents just before Shabbat through Ambulance Klein. We bought many things for the baby; with two salaries it seemed easy. Life in Israel seemed comfortable and good; the economy was stable and growing. Emma came home after two or three days, and we settled into a new routine. She decided, and I agreed, to call the boy Ariel Shmuel; she had an uncle Ariel and Shmuel was her father's name. The Brit was in Tel Hashomer and my father was the Sandak, or person holding the baby. In Sephardi tradition, one can call the baby by his grandfather's name even if the grandfather is alive, while in Ashkenazi one can only do so after the person is deceased.

After a few months' maternity leave, Emma went back to work and we hired a nanny. Celia lost her first pregnancy, but in October '72 she gave birth to Mali. Then Emma became pregnant again, too soon. Ariel was a lively baby and later an active toddler; we took him often to nearby Kfar Hamaccabiah, which had trees, grass, a pool and other facilities. As Emma's pregnancy advanced, it became impossible for her to change Ariel's nappies as he would wriggle away. Emma used to call me to come home from work to change him, then go immediately back to work. While I was in miluim, we had the second boy and Emma, again I agreed, called him Amos; his second name was Pinchas after my mother's father. Based on Talmudic tradition, I planted a tree when each of the boys was born; the Talmud gave specific trees, different for boys and girls, but I liked the tree called Pilpelon or Little Pepper. On each trip to Shafir, we used to check the trees; one was doing better but I don't remember whose. The tradition was to cut branches from the tree for the Chupah of the child, but by the time Ariel got married the house had been sold and the new owners had cut down all the trees. It was great for my father that we had two boys so that the family name would be carried on. We often visited my parents and they often visited us; there was clearly a bond between my father and Ariel – as soon as baby Ariel saw my father, he would stand up and stretch out his arms as a sign that he wanted my father to pick him up. Ariel must have sensed how much my father felt about him. My father was now able to buy things that he hadn't been able to in the past and he would buy sweets and try to give them to me, but I did not want them as I had got used to life without sweets. Emma's parents also visited about twice a year, staying half the time with us and half the time with Celia and Julio. During Shabbat, we all usually ate together, also when Emma's parents were away. Not long after Ariel's birth, I had an eye test and was told I should wear glasses; it seemed the prediction by the air force eye doctor in 1965 was correct. But after some thirty years of wearing glasses, I was told that I didn't need them; should I try the air force again now? Ahh, I'll wait a few years.

Around this time, Emma's parents with two of Emma's father's sisters decided to share a flat in Israel, and I found a penthouse for them in a nine-storey block being built not far from us. I decided it was time to move away from Hayarden Street, which was becoming too noisy, and we agreed to buy a flat in the same building. I decided on the fifth floor so that on Shabbat and festivals it would be easier to go up to the ninth floor without the lift. Emma was sensitive to the cold, so I paid for under-floor heating, which left no money for allocated registered parking, which I regretted years later. The process of buying or selling a property was quite straightforward; we advertised the flat in the small ad pages of one of the papers and a family wanted to buy it. They put down a deposit and we wrote and signed a Zichron Dvarim, or basics of the agreement. Later we used a lawyer to draft a full agreement. Our new flat was in a building off Hayarden street, in an area that used to be an orchard but was being swallowed up by the expanding city at the expense of green areas. The building was one of the first to be built in that district, and for years there were large open spaces where the children could run around and play. They brought in a lot of sand in their shoes and I had to sweep it up, as Emma was not so good at it. The best times were during Lag BaOmer when, to commemorate the end of a plague that killed thousands of pupils nearly two millennia ago, children arranged bonfires. The wood for the fires was 'borrowed' from the many building sites in the area. Ramat Gan, the name of our city, meant Garden Heights, but with so many new buildings, I called it a concrete jungle.

MOVING TO THE UK

With Emma working at university, it made sense for her to do a doctorate to enable her to progress. She made arrangements and we decided to go to England for three years so she could do the degree. My idea was that we'd sell the flat in Hayarden Street and store our belongings while the new flat in Sderat Kam was being built. I would benefit financially as there would be a difference in price between a flat sold immediately and a flat delivered in a year's time. We stored some items at my parents' and some in a room in the new flat, even though it was still being built. There was a lot of running around to do with our and Emma' parents' and aunts' new flats, as the contractor provided only basic kitchen and bathrooms. In August '73, Emma with the two boys and with Rivka and her teenage daughter, Liela, flew to London. Rivka and her daughter were to help Emma, but their suitcases were left behind, so they spent a long time at El Al's desk. Emma had taken her accumulated studying fund from the university of about £1,000 in cash and had it in her bag. With the little boys needing attention, she did not guard her bag, which was on the El Al desk. When she unpacked at her parents' home, where everyone was staying, she discovered that the money had disappeared. The El Al clerk denied taking it, but the money we were relying on to live during the first few months had gone.

I started to work at Dun and Bradstreet in London, which took me on recommendation of the Israeli office. I was soon disappointed, as the work was totally different from what we did in Israel. In Israel we did in-depth analysis and reports, but in London the reports were superficial and relied mainly on publicly available information. There was a lot of laughter in the office when it snowed, and I went to the window to see snow fall for the first time. Colleagues could not believe I had never seen it; it looked to me like lots of feathers in swirls. I had seen snow on the ground when I was twenty; I was in the army and we heard on the news that snow was falling in Jerusalem, so a group of us travelled from the south to see it. My colleagues at Dun and Bradstreet also did not understand why I asked when Christmas was; I had to explain that in Israel there are many Christian sects, which celebrate Christmas on different dates; during the month of December at the end of the news, the newsreader would frequently say something like 'today was the Christmas of the X Christian sect'. I also had difficulty with directions of Earth: when I went out of the house I grew up in, I faced east, but in London when I went out I faced north. I knew it but it still felt as if I was facing east.

A two-day weekend was new to me too, and I started to have migraines nearly every Sunday, especially rainy ones when I could not go out with the boys. I realised the reason was that I was used to a one-day weekend, only on the Shabbat; so every Sunday I would do some do-it-yourself task or gardening, and the migraines disappeared. I still do gardening work as it keeps my contact with nature and reminds me of my youth in Shafir. A few days after I started work, the Yom Kippur War broke out and my parents did not want me to come back; anyway, we had no money for a ticket. Given the way the Six Day War was won, I like most others expected Israel to win quickly; but the news was bad, and we started to see many Israeli prisoners of war. I felt guilty being away and tried to follow the news as much as possible. This war was so different and, even though Israeli soldiers came nearer Cairo and Damascus in the end, early setbacks and the number of casualties meant that no one in Israel celebrated victory. Long-term consequences of the war

– peace with Egypt and the end of the Labour party's control of government – manifested themselves a few years later when we were living again in Israel. After 1973 there were no further wars between Israel and any Arab state.

At some stage I started to feel that my mother was hiding something from me. During one telephone conversation – she used the telephone at Ambulance Klein's home – I pressed her and she told me my father had cancer. I could not stand. Everything was turning around and I was very upset. My parents still insisted I should not come; nothing was all right for me, and there was more to come.

In the meantime, I had problems with the sale of the flat in Hayarden Street and purchase of our new one in Ramat Gan. The buyer was called up to the army and did not have to pay me while in active service, but I was abroad and not serving in the army, so I had to continue with my payments. Since my payment schedule relied on receipts from the purchaser of my flat, I had to pay penalty interest. The contractor was well-off and understood my predicament and was quite reasonable. When I came to Israel months later, the neighbours at 22 Hayarden Street told me that the army had come looking for me on Yom Kippur itself. The war was not going well, and I was also worried about my father. At some stage my aunt and uncle said I should come back; my father-in-law lent me the money for the flight and I took unpaid leave from work. My father seemed to be coping with his ordeal and Menachem Schlesinger, Rafi's older brother, who worked as a doctor in the Kaplan hospital in Rehovot, where my father was, told me that he was present at the operation and, while a growth on the kidney was the size of a football, the cancer was all in one place and had not spread. This was the first time my father had been in hospital. My mother and I visited every day; it went on for about two weeks. One day my father asked if he could see the grandchildren, forgetting that they were in London; ever since, I wished he could have seen them. A few days later we came in and went to the room where he was, together with about ten other patients, and he was not there. He'd been moved to the intensive care unit, where he was wired to machines and very unhappy. We didn't know why his condition had deteriorated; I think he had suffered so much in his life that he just could not overcome another hurdle. My mother and I stayed now all the time. Every so often I was crying and pretended that I had to do something to one of the instruments so that my father would not see. My father also cried from time to time; one felt demoralised and helpless. He died the next day; I phoned my aunt and we just cried and cried until my tokens for the public phone finished. I was so angry with God and everything in the world. My father had had such a difficult life and, just when he started to have a better time and enjoy himself, he was taken away, aged only sixty-nine. We buried him the next day in the local cemetery. The boys have no memory of him, which is fair enough given their age when he died, but it is very upsetting for me.

My aunt sat shiva with us. One day I noticed my mother throwing away papers. When I asked what she was doing, she said my father kept too many old documents. I rescued and still have most of them; some of the information in this memoir, mainly about early years, comes from them. My mother did not feel sentimental as I do. I mentioned the one hundred china pieces my grandmother received for her wedding; a few had broken during or before the journey to Israel. On one of my later visits there I noticed the number of pieces had gone down further; I asked my mother what had happened and she said she gave them as gifts when she was invited to weddings, as she had little money. I was upset and said I would give her money for gifts but she was not to give away more of the china. Similarly on one of my trips, I could not find my old bicycle; my mother had given it to the paid night guard from Zrachia, in lieu of his clearing round the house. I was upset but said nothing as my mother needed his help. When my parents-in-law came to Israel on a usual biannual visit, I took them to my father's grave. The cemetery is for five local religious villages and near the military base Julis, with an uninterrupted view all the way to the Judaean mountains. My father-in-law noted the view instantly and commented on how beautiful it was.

On return to London I changed jobs, moving to a small firm of chartered accountants. There was a short cut to the office via Smithfield meat market and I, who had never seen a pig in Israel, now saw hundreds of them each day slaughtered and hanging on hooks. Life for an observant person is simpler in Israel: all non-meat products are kosher, and the life cycle is based on the Jewish calendar. I like to keep the Shabbat holy and separate from other days; you can call it religion, observance, tradition or just a way to put boundaries around one's time so as not to be consumed by quotidiana. The idea of a day of rest must have been revolutionary in ancient times, but it is even more relevant today, as modern life can be so stressful. Another difference between my life in London and life in Israel is that, if any name came up in the media that was Jewish, Emma's family would discuss it. I later noticed that nearly every Jew did the same, over both positive and negative coverage. Perhaps it is because Jews in the diaspora are a minority and so see every Jew, especially high-profile Jews, as representing or at least casting a reflection on all the community.

c. 1970s

BACK TO ISRAEL

Once we realised Emma was not going to complete her doctorate soon, I wanted to get back to Israel. So in the late summer of '76, I returned ahead of Emma and the children and arranged a few immediate job interviews. I had an offer from the Internal Audit department of Bank Hapoalim and started work within two or three days of my arrival. We settled into the new flat at 6 Sderat Kam in Ramat Gan with Celia's family just round the corner. Most of our neighbours were young couples; one exception was the Margulins, who lived directly below us on the fourth floor. The wife, Miri, was a sister of Ben Zion Netanyahu, father of Yoni, killed in the hostage rescue from Entebbe, and Bibi, the future prime minister. Ariel settled in very quickly while Amos was more reserved and spent most of his time with his cousins Mali and Tiri. I used to take them to the Gan, or nursery, then go on to work. Ariel had already been to a nursery in London, where he had to wear a tie, so he insisted on wearing a tie to the Gan, but it was tucked in so not so visible. This did not last long as children like to blend into the society they live in. My mother often visited us, and we stayed at weekends with her. I used to go after work at about 15:30 (we started at 07:30) to the famous Shuk Hacarmel or Carmel market in Tel Aviv and buy bags of fresh fruit and vegetables. As for bedtime stories, I did not want to read English stories, so nearly every night I would invent a new story, usually about wild animals, which were popular with the boys.

Cars were expensive in Israel, so we were only able to afford a small old Subaru. It gave me a lot of trouble and, once I was entitled to a loan from the bank, I bought an Italian Autobianchi, also second-hand and small but much better than the Subaru. For a family with children it is difficult to manage without a car in Israel. I was happy with work and doing well. I was never able to figure out my salary since it had so many one-off and different components, but I did not care as it was always more than I expected. On top of this, we received share options; the shares were blocked for five years so I started to benefit only a half-decade after I joined the bank. Overall, bank employees in Israel, in those days at least, had a high income, and the only thing I checked was if I was paying tax at the top rate. The bank was run by Ya'akov Levinson, a talented and powerful man on the Israeli economic and political scene. The audit department was an example of a typical problem faced by Bank Hapoalim. Half the department was made up of older people who were clerks in the Histadrut, or trade union, and its many affiliates; most did not think they should work hard and probably were not capable of working hard. The other half were new employees, young university graduates who were ambitious and willing to work hard. The older employees thought they had rights first and obligations last. I remember one who used to take a day off each month as 'sick' even though he was not sick. He would conveniently interpret the bank's permission merely to sign a declaration if one was sick for one day and did not see a doctor. Levinson's task was to modernise the bank. It was a problem faced also by the government and all trade union affiliated businesses, as Israel was a heavily socialist economy. The trade union was also one of the biggest employers in the country, second only to the state itself.

The founding fathers of Israel had a mammoth task, to absorb millions of immigrants, mostly unskilled, and create a viable economy without natural resources and with high defence costs. On the whole, in my opinion, they did it right, but it was time to move on from a regime of protecting local employment at all costs and stifling entrepreneurship. Levinson succeeded in modernising Bank Hapoalim, and it replaced Bank Leumi as the largest bank in the country. My speciality was loans and credits. In my second year at the bank, I was auditing the Montefiore branch in Tel Aviv, which was five minutes' walk from the audit department offices in Allenby Street. On Friday in those days we finished, like most office workers, at one o'clock, so the traffic leaving central Tel Aviv at one was a disaster. One Friday around noon, I noticed a possible big error in a large complex loan granted to one of the trade union affiliated companies. I stayed on checking but then the branch was closing, so I had to leave. All weekend the loan was going through my mind and I waited for Sunday morning to finish my investigation; at that time everything was stored on microfiche or computer printout. After checking, I was sure that my hunch had been correct and millions of Lirot had not been collected from the borrower. I knew I was onto something and walked to the office to tell the deputy head of department what I'd discovered. A very experienced person came back with me to the branch to confirm my findings. The audit department deputy head wrote a report, which was hand-delivered to the chairman, Levinson. The head of department and his deputy were excited about my find as it was ammunition in their fight with the bank's department for human resources. I'd found millions for the bank. The branch had been confused since the computers then only gave indications about repayment of index-linked loans; if repayment was delayed, the amount would change, inflation in Israel being so high. This loan was complex and to complicate the indexation calculations, capital repayment started only five years after drawdown. Ironically, the customer had told the bank it was making a mistake and should charge more, but the branch had ignored him because it misunderstood its own computer reports. The company had created a reserve for the undercharging and, based on my discoveries, paid all that was due. This prompted the bank to advance an upgrade of its computerisation of indexation calculations. In order to find what I'd found, one had to work hard and be lucky. I already had a good reputation for dealing with complex loans, but this was in a class of its own, and most importantly Levinson noticed. I remember that some of my colleagues used to say that if they got more money or a promotion they would work harder, but it actually goes the other way: if you work harder, then you are more likely to be promoted.

Emma did not find it easy in Israel. This was partly at least because she did not want to settle there. She found it difficult when the children started to speak English with a Hebrew accent; and when she asked for directions, people would sometimes move on without replying. Everyone knows that Israelis are rude, but the main reason Emma did not get responses was that her questions were too long. She would say something like 'Excuse me I want to go to...' but if you want to ask how to get somewhere in Israel, you just shout out the name of the place and an answer will come. I saw old friends mainly when we stayed over Shabbat at my mother's and friends did the same at their parents' homes. Emma found it difficult to blend in and penetrate Israeli social groupings. We did mix socially with some work colleagues, both hers and mine, also with some neighbours and parents of friends of our children. Emma was teaching both at Tel Aviv University and privately, and with the bank's salary we were able to breathe financially. Because of the high inflation I, like most people, converted my salary into bank shares or foreign currency on the day of receipt. This meant that most of the time we were in overdraft, which grew towards the end of each month. Emma found this frightening and hated it. Israel's annual inflation went from 31% in 1976 to 76% in 1979 and by 1984 reached 450%. In the '70s, Israeli banks were technologically more advanced than British banks; for example, one was able to print a statement which was updated to the minute.

SADAT VISIT

During this period of living in Israel, there were some dramatic events. First of all, Begin won the general election; it was the first time that the Labour party in its various forms did not win an election since the foundation of the state. Then there was Sadat's visit and the peace agreement. I don't like politics and most politicians, so I do not follow the news in detail, but everything surrounding that visit on 19 November 1977 interested me. Before explaining, a short detour: Israeli sport did not succeed on the international stage; an exception was the Maccabi Tel Aviv basketball team which, in April 1977, won the European Championship under the guidance of its legendry captain, Tal Brodie. The evening of the victory, Rabin announced that he was not going to be a candidate for prime minister, but no one paid attention; the whole country was celebrating. I remember Zeev's cartoons in *Haaretz*: in one, the streets are deserted, everyone glued to TV, even the traffic lights bending towards a window to watch the game; in another, Rabin is trying to tell the masses celebrating outside, 'Stop the country, I want to get off' but no one is paying attention.

As mentioned earlier, we gave the TV we purchased to my parents. We were unusual in not having one: our children had to go to cousins or friends to watch anything. But just before Sadat arrived, I was excited by the prospect of peace and following the news in detail, so I rented a TV. I was and am a pacifist in my nature and beliefs; it was circumstances that made me go to the army and participate in wars. If Israel did not have a strong military, it would not exist; I don't agree that in Israel people should not serve in the military on the ground that they are pacifists. This would be asking someone else to protect their family, and no one can opt out in matters of life and death.

As the peace process dragged on, I actually bought a TV. The Camp David accords were signed on 17 September 1978; this led to a treaty between Israel and Egypt signed on 26 March 1979. It did not surprise me that a right-wing politician was the one who signed a treaty giving Sinai back to the Egyptians. The logic is that any peace agreement presented by a left-leaning party will be rejected by right-leaning parties but when the opposite occurs, the left-leaning parties will support it. There was strong opposition to giving Sinai back from right wing groups in Israel, and some of those living in Yamit, in Sinai and their supporters had to be removed by force. Earlier in 1977, I had taken my parents-in-law to visit Yamit; it was the only town I ever saw that was built well. The centre was for pedestrians only and the buildings were attractive and situated so that they did not block a breeze from the sea. Most of the towns in Israel are built badly and breeze from the sea, so important in a hot country, is blocked by ugly tall buildings. Yamit was bulldozered to the ground before it was handed to Egypt.

On 10 December 1978, both Begin and Sadat received the Nobel peace prize. I believe Sadat was the first Moslem to win a Nobel prize. It is interesting to note that Egypt did not want Gaza back; they wanted every inch of the nearly empty Sinai desert, but they did not want even an inch of the overpopulated strip. Begin, on the other hand, was proud that he had 'saved' Gaza for Israel; he considered the strip part of Eretz Israel, or the Land of Israel, but not the Sinai. I wonder what Begin would say today given the continuing conflict between Israel and Hamas, which rules Gaza. Sadly, Sadat was assassinated by army officers on 6 October 1981 during a military parade to commemorate the '73 war. The media instantly connected the assassination to Sadat's peace with Israel two and half years earlier, and the connection has remained ever since. What I recall is that the assassins said they killed Sadat because he was not a devout enough Muslim and promoted western not Muslim values. Obviously, the Israeli-Egyptian peace treaty was a factor, but the assassins might have killed him regardless.

A side effect of the Yom Kippur war, when Israel lost nearly a third of its front-line combat planes, coupled with its dependency on other countries for weapons to defend itself, was that the government decided in 1980 to build from scratch its own fighter plane. This was a controversial decision as the project would swallow a large part of the defence budget, which was very high in terms of GDP. The plane was called Lavi or lion; it created much needed jobs and was a prestige project for a small country; Israelis were proud of their nation's capability. But seven years later, after building two prototypes (first flight 31/12/1986) the government, under heavy pressure from the US, which did not want competition, voted 12 to 11 to cancel the project. Like many, I was disappointed: the plane would have been unique to Israel and most suitable to its requirements; French and American planes owned by Israel were owned also by Arab countries. With hindsight, it was the right decision: the project was too big for a small country. That said, it did help Israel to launch its first space satellite in 1988, and it laid the foundation for a successful aviation industry, especially in unmanned drones. Coincidentally or not, China's first home-built fighter plane, the J10, which was unveiled in 1998, was very similar to the Lavi.

LONDON AGAIN

After three years at the bank, I moved in 1979 to London as Internal Auditor of its UK branches. I reported to one of five joint Chief executives, Chaim Bergstein. I had a large office and was told clearly that I was *not* reporting to Eliezer Teomi, the bank's overall Internal Auditor – typical internal politics. On 23 April 1980 I received a letter from Ya'akov Levinson saying that, in accordance with a decision of the bank's board of management, I was from now on to report to the undersigned – i.e., Levinson himself. I was gobsmacked; I was thirty-three years old, reporting direct to the chairman of the biggest bank in Israel, one of the most powerful men in the country. I still have the original letter and other correspondence with him. Levinson showed an interest in what I was doing and before his frequent visits to the UK, one of his secretaries would send me a telex asking if I would be available to meet him at some precise time like 14:55. Of course I always replied instantly 'yes'. He did use me for some of his games: for example, while I was in his room, he would call Bergstein or Ya'akov Geva, another joint chief executive, asking them to call so and so. I did not like this, as he used the chief executives as messengers in my presence, and I was worried that they would punish me somehow, as I had witnessed their humiliation.

BACK TO ISRAEL ALONE

Levinson decided to leave the bank and move to the US to run Ampal, an investment holding company, and Giura Gazit was appointed the new chairman. He ignored me – I suppose in his eyes I was Levinson's man – and in the summer of '81 the bank told me that it was time for me to return to Israel. As my late father-in-law said, 'Now there arose a new king over Egypt, who knew not Joseph'. I contacted Teomi, the bank's internal auditor, and he promised to appoint me his deputy. Emma said she was not going back to Israel, so I decided to go alone, in the hope that my career in the bank would continue to progress and she would follow. Teomi did not renege on his promise but started to play for time. Levinson was in all the papers in Israel, as Rabin and Peres, competing to be Labour leader, wanted him to be on their side, with the promise to appoint him finance minister if they won the next election, giving him a wide range of authority. In the end Levinson declined, as Peres beat Rabin for the leadership and did not agree to give him all the powers he wanted. Later accusations surfaced that Levinson had been involved in financial mismanagement while head of Bank Hapoalim. Many articles and a few books were written on this sad topic, and my predecessor as internal auditor of the bank's UK operation is mentioned in at least one of them. I personally have no doubt that Levinson did not steal money; I remember an article in *Maariv* by Ehud Olmert, later Israel's prime minister, in which he also wrote that he believed that Levinson did not take anything for his own gain. (As I mention Olmert, I want to add that I thought he was a good prime minister; it was a shame how his career ended.) Levinson was not motivated by money, he was motivated by power. He may have made inappropriate financial transactions relating to the assets of the Histadrut, or trade union, but not for himself. The background to this was the unexpected win of Begin in the '77 election and Labour's fear that Begin's party would put their hand on Histadrut assets; so in complex transactions Levinson probably moved asset ownership into structures that would give the Labour Party control over them. Levinson could not face the huge change in his fortunes; I was told by a person from the bank who knew him well that he was depressed, and he ended by committing suicide on 26 February 1984. I was very upset. He was talented and did not deserve such an end.

Once I had been abroad for over a year, my army unit returned me, so to speak, to the general pool; the fact that they had not been able to call me up for reserve duty had put an extra burden on other members of the unit. During my earlier return to Israel, I had been trained as a medic. When I came back this time, I was allocated to a new unit, a serious tank unit, and called up quite often, always to serve on the Golan Heights. One such tour of duty was along the border with Lebanon. The border fence had sensitive sensors and, whenever anything crossed, they would raise an alarm. We would rush to the spot and the tracker, a Bedouin Arab, would get out of the vehicle, check footprints and return saying a single word in Arabic, which meant wild animal, after which we would return to base to sleep until the next alarm. Luckily, there were no crossings by humans or any excitement during my tour. As this area was a nature reserve, it was stunning; no doubt it still is, but it is not open to the public. There were many different wild animals; I recall foxes with big, beautiful tails sneaking into the small base to scavenge. Another tour of duty was by the border with Syria, in a very sensitive spot on Mt. Hermon, the 'eyes' and 'ears' of Israel. It was nerve-wracking to be on guard duty there. On one occasion my and my colleagues' caused an explosion – but don't get alarmed: it was to do with cooking. We were in this remote area and supply came only once a week and there was no cook, as we probably were not enough in numbers to qualify for one. One Friday we decided to cook the traditional Shabbat food: Cholent. We had all the ingredients, but we put in the eggs at the wrong time. They exploded inside the saucepan; however, as this was the first cooked meal we had had for days, we did not give up and spent most of Shabbat picking and removing bits of eggshell. As far as I remember the Cholent was great, but I don't remember if this was because we were desperate for cooked food or that it was really good.

I had returned to Israel full of hope, but the reality turned out different. With Teomi playing games, the family far off and maintaining two homes taking its toll, I asked Emma at the beginning of 1982 to come for a while and, if it did not work out, we would all go back to London. Emma agreed to come for six months and arrived with the boys in the spring. Ariel re-joined his class at Moreshet Moshe school and Amos also joined the school. Amos ignored all the lessons except maths, at which he was very good. While I was on my own this time, I had shaved off the beard I'd started to grow because of lack of time when I was a student, and everyone said I looked more like how I had looked at my youth. I'd started to become grey relatively early and the partly white beard added years to my age. But at the airport when I met Emma, Ariel and Amos on arrival, both Emma and Ariel insisted I go back to growing a beard, so I did. When Emma and her friends talked about hair colouring, I used to say that I colour my hair white, and pointed to the evidence, my grey hair, saying that I do it so that people will take me more seriously. It did not help; not everything I said or say today is taken seriously. This is partly my fault as I tell people never to believe anything I say, including this sentence.

FIRST LEBANON WAR

Then there was the first Lebanon war, which was very unpleasant. Emma wrote an article about it for *The Jewish Chronicle* in June 2012, thirtieth anniversary of the war. She believes that my experiences then changed me, but I don't agree with her. The story starts earlier, during a routine miluim service, as usual on the Golan Heights, in the winter of '81/2. After some incident in the Jordan valley, a shooting or crossing from Jordan near Mechola, where my friend Israel Nedivi lives, we were told to prepare for big action. Everyone guessed that Sharon, then defence minister, meant to use the incident as an excuse to invade Lebanon to fight the Palestinians there, but three or four days of heavy rain made invasion impossible. For some years, a weak government in Lebanon had been unable to control these Palestinians, who had moved there in 1948 or after being thrown out of Jordan in September 1970; they had created a state within a state, and civil war had begun in 1975. The next incident to invite invasion came in June 1982, when the Israeli Ambassador to the UK, Shlomo Argov, was shot and badly wounded. When I heard that news, I told Emma there was going to be war; and indeed Israel invaded Lebanon on 6 June. I was quite happy not to be called up instantly, but two days into the war I was traced and asked why I did not report to my unit. It transpired that the call-up papers had been sent to my previous address. So I left Emma, Ariel aged ten and Amos aged nine and travelled to Kurdany near Akko, where a few other colleagues from my unit who'd missed the call-up were gathering. We signed for our personal gear (very heavy) and were taken by lorry to one of the mountains north of Tsfat, to await orders.

The war came at a bad time for me – not that there ever is a good time for war. Unlike Israelis, Emma did not have the experience or infrastructure to cope with a situation when her husband was off in a war. She had two young children and, added to that, she did not agree with the war. I also did not agree that the war was an 'ein brera', or a 'no choice' war, inevitable if Israel were to survive; but I was the only one in my unit to think so – everyone else was absolutely in favour of it. Emma and I, without sharing the fact between us, each kept a diary during the war: everything was so different from the Six Day War.

I normally would call my mother every day, but I could not call from Lebanon; so after not hearing from me for two days, she called our home. Ariel answered and told her I was on a business trip; the ten-year-old felt the sensitivities and knew she would be in a state if she knew I'd been called up. If Emma had answered the phone, she would have told the truth. Anyway, my mother realised it a few days later.

Early in the morning on the third day of the war, after sleeping under the sky near Tsfat, we crossed into Lebanon with the aim of joining our unit. At the time of crossing, one wonders how it is going to be and if one is going to come back, but as we drove through the Lebanese villages we were surprised at how welcoming the people were, throwing rice at us, apparently a sign of welcome, and flowers. These locals had suffered from the Palestinians and would be happy to have them driven away. We drove east to the Bekaa Valley, then north and then west, chasing our unit in vain and ending the day in the refinery area of Sidon on the Mediterranean. It was hot; flies and enormous mosquitoes also welcomed us, but without flowers. I was used to Israeli mosquitoes and probably immune to them, but we really suffered from the Lebanese ones. Although

Lebanon is the only country in the Middle East that does not have a desert, we were totally covered in dust and went to the sea to wash. At this stage, we ate manot krav or prepacked food boxes for times of war, with tins and other unpleasant items. My diary records: 'By Saturday, just the sight of the food made me feel sick, so I ate nothing on Saturday and Sunday. Then we started to receive presents and letters sent by children and since then we have been eating only chocolates and sweets. I assume I shall be sick of this soon. I was touched by the packets sent by the children. Luckily no one wrote to us, as had happened in the past, 'I hope you will die a hero for our country''. There were many stray dogs, I suppose as a result of seven years of civil war. We gladly gave the dogs our tinned food and I noticed that they ate some of it and buried the rest. I had never noticed such a phenomenon in Israel and was wondering if the Lebanese dogs had learnt the necessity of saving for a rainy day. Drinking water came with us, towed by the vehicles.

After a day, we drove straight north on the coastal road to the outskirts of Beirut, where we finally met up with our unit. The area we drove through was attractive, a narrow pass between hills and sea with lots of fruit trees. At some point during the drive we were told that Syrian planes were heading our way and we had to close the top of the armoured vehicle. In the end, the planes never got close; nevertheless, the experience was not pleasant as we felt very exposed and vulnerable to air attacks. The first time we were fired on was on the outskirts of Beirut, and it was decided that we should locate away from the front line. We drove back south a few kilometres to Damour, where we created a field hospital in a deserted villa. It seemed to me that Damour was a mostly deserted upmarket village, with many of its villas apparently belonging to sheikhs from the Gulf, who had stopped visiting since the outbreak of civil war. We were told that the estate where we were had once belonged to the Shah of Iran. The main house was built attractively but stripped of everything; we saw broken leftover beautiful tiles in the corners of what were the kitchen and bathrooms. There were a few additional buildings and a swimming pool full of rubbish. The sea was close by; to get there we had to cross an unused railway line originally built by the British to connect Beirut with Haifa.

Casualties started to come in. I remember well the first dead soldier, a paratrooper, but not any of the others. I recalled that after the Six Day War, when passing a kindergarten in Ashkelon, I had thought that, given the scale of the victory, how lucky the children were as they would not face wars anymore; but those children of '67 were now fighting, and some dying. We treated civilians too and were fired on a few times. I remember going to war-torn Beirut airport, but don't recall why. From where I was, Beirut seemed much like Tel Aviv, especially the many blocks of flats. Some soldiers visited the local village and were warmly welcomed and shown round; they came back impressed with stories about sunken baths with gold taps. Apparently, the locals they saw were servants, as the owners who lived there, like the sheiks from the Gulf, had moved abroad. A group of the soldiers did something forbidden: they brought back chocolates and fizzy drinks they'd 'borrowed' from a shop they had broken into. I read in my diary that I was angry with them. At one point Begin, the prime minister was visiting the US, and Simcha Erlich, the acting prime minister, announced that there were no Israeli soldiers in Beirut. This was typical of Sharon, who did whatever he wanted and misled his superiors.

More from my diary: '16.6.82. Today was the first day I looked in a mirror. I think that, apart from the full beard, you will recognise me. 17.6.82. I am desperate to know how you, and everyone are. I do not even know whether you have received anything from me or not. I have now finished my shift at the reception and treatment area. We are more settled here; there is an electricity generator and even a TV, but we can only see Lebanese programmes. We have a good view of Beirut and it was surprising to notice at night that the lights were on. This past night, also, we were shelled and bombed... Even the thick walls of our building were shaking. I was surprised to realise that I was not frightened or affected. Two dead soldiers were brought in, but I did not see them. We had mainly sick soldiers and civilians. One prisoner was brought in; he had a bullet through his leg, and it was obvious that he must have been wounded days ago but had only now given himself up. He said he was a Syrian soldier but people speaking Arabic to him were sure he was just a local terrorist. Later he was moved south.'

There was no possibility of contacting the family. I had vicarious contact, as I wrote the diary in the form of letters to Emma. After about ten days some people, chosen by lottery, were allowed to visit home. After three weeks I and others were demobilised and eight of us got into a civilian Ford transit van, which was also being demobbed, to drive back to Israel – in those days vehicles and equipment were still called on for reserve duty. We were driving south on the same coastal road we had driven north three weeks earlier; at some point, we heard a bang and saw a cloud of sand blown up; an RPG (rocket propelled grenade) fired at us had missed by inches. The driver pressed the accelerator of the flimsy van as hard as he could; we stopped at the first check point and reported the incident. A few inches lower and all eight of us in the unprotected van would have been dead. This was very real; I may have at other times been in a dangerous situation, as I served in Lebanon a few times during 1982 and 1983, but did not realise it. We crossed back into Israel at Rosh Hanikra and a few hours later arrived home. An important point for me: I never fired in anger, so I am sure I never killed or even wounded anyone.

This comes from Emma's diary: 'Sunday, I received my first communication from Chaim. In the form of an army postcard written in Hebrew. I rushed to a neighbour to have it read to me. Apart from saying that he was fine, and not saying where he was, the main piece of information was that I shouldn't expect him to phone. While that gave me the 'go ahead' to leave the flat in the afternoon, rather than making a point of staying in as I had done most of the previous week, I immediately regretted my absence from home that evening when my son told me, on my return, that a man had called about daddy 'from the army'. I was only mildly reassured by the one piece of information he had clearly understood: 'hu margish tov' – he feels okay. That apart, Ariel was confused and spoke of 'a man with a bullet through his leg' and the possibility of his father 'being a prisoner'. Ariel was under the impression that the man would call back, so we waited, sick with tension, for the phone to ring.' I have no idea who the person that rang was; he must have been unclear or the line was bad as Ariel's Hebrew is quite good.

As mentioned, this was not a war of 'no choice' like the wars of '48, '67 and '73, and this time the country was divided. Then in September 1982 came the massacre of Palestinians in the Sabra and Shatila neighbourhoods of Beirut by Christian Phalangists in revenge for the assassination of their leader, Bashir Gemayel. The

Palestinians should have been protected by the Israeli army, and there were huge demonstrations in Israel against the government. About ten percent of Israel's adult population attended the demonstration in Kikar Malchei Israel in Tel Aviv, demanding the resignation of Begin and Sharon. The demonstrators also demanded an independent judicial enquiry into Israel's role. On 28 September an enquiry was set up headed by Yitzhak Kahan, the president of the Supreme Court. The enquiry found that the Israeli army should have foreseen the possibility of the massacre, and Sharon and some army officers had to resign. In the meantime, I was called up again and again to miluim in different parts of Lebanon. Altogether I would spend nearly six months there. In the winter of 1983, I was in the Chouf Mountains, covered in snow. After our initial welcome in June, the attitude of the local population had turned against us. It was dangerous to be in Lebanon, and soldiers were killed and wounded. A soldier from my unit was killed in the Chouf by the locals, who were Druze; they just shot at him as if they were hunting animals. We were flown into and out of Lebanon. I had been flown in the past to the air force base Refidim in Sinai to do miluim, but this was different; then there had been no danger, and a Boeing 707 was used. A side note: during the miluim in Refidim, I was a little jealous of the pilots; the fighter planes, so deadly and powerful, looked to me flimsy except when they were taking off – the earth nearby shook, and fire seemed to come out of the engine. To Lebanon, however, we were flown by military transport aircraft which could land and take off on short, rough runways; we sat on folding chairs along the fuselage with equipment in the middle. We were unable to see anything as there were no windows, and lack of insulation made the engine noise deafening. I was glad when we landed in the small Haifa airport. Since this war, I never agreed to watch any war movies.

I have photos from the war and from the miluim services, but I want to reiterate that, from the start, both Emma and I were against the war. Friends and family were divided; for Emma it was difficult that her close relatives were for the war. As it happened, nearly all the men in the building we lived in were not called up, and Emma complained that so many people were not called up when her husband was. My mother did go to the military office (ktzin hair) dealing with families of people called up to try and plead for me to come home, but obviously her reasoning was not good enough.

Emma's father knew a few well-known Israelis – one was the legendry Abba Eban; I had taken my father-in-law to Eban's house in Hertzlia Pituch. Others were the right-wing activists: Elyakim HaEtzni, who was a founder of Kiriyat Arabba, the Jewish town near Hebron, and Harry Hurwitz, an adviser to Begin who wrote his biography. During one of my miluim services, HaEtzni came to visit my father-in-law; Emma waited until late before going to see her parents, assuming that by then HaEtzni would have left. But he had not; as it happened, one of the leaders of Fatah had been assassinated that day, and HaEtzni was happy about it. I was told by Julio, my brother-in-law, that when Emma arrived and heard HaEtzni, she argued with him forcefully, not forgetting to tell him that she spoke as someone whose husband was serving right then in Lebanon.

During some of those miluim services, I had short visits home and Ariel was intrigued with the gun and other equipment I had. On one service, the army had its first large-scale exercise after the war, on the Golan Heights. I disliked it, and it did not help that my nagmash, or armoured people's carrier, was located near Ariel Sharon and his entourage. I was surprised how the obese Sharon was so mobile; he jumped on rocks and did not stay still for one minute, but the halo of the brave paratrooper had gone. Sorry, I never liked him; but who knows, as a member of the right wing, he might have brought peace had he not gone into a coma in January 2006, after a stroke from which he never recovered. I remember reading an article by Uri Dan, a paratrooper turned journalist, saying that those who objected and blocked Sharon from becoming the army chief of staff got him as defence minister, those who objected to him as defence minister would get him as prime minister, and later it came true. As prime minister, Sharon decided and executed in 2005 disengagement from Gaza and part of the northern West Bank. I knew a few families from my moshav and nearby moshavim living in the Gaza strip. Some American Jews bought the greenhouses left by these settlers and gave them to the Palestinians, who demolished them and used their location to fire rockets into Israel. At some stage Israel retreated from most of Lebanon, remaining only in a security zone, but under pressure from large parts of Israeli society and constant guerrilla fighting with Hezbollah, Israel finally left totally in 2000. Too many Israeli soldiers had died, including a son of a friend and one from Shafir. The Lebanon episode left scars on many soldiers and, even after physically leaving Lebanon it did not leave them. My Lebanon experience turned me against the invasion of Iraq by the US and UK in 2003, not because I was pro Saddam Hussein but because I knew that nothing could come of it except blood, tears and suffering. I did not join anti-war demonstrations in London, however, because they also became anti-Israel.

Unlike my years of service between the ages of eighteen and twenty-one, my miluim services were very tough and I served long periods of them. I could write separate chapters about each, but will refer only to kur hahituch, or melting-pot, again re these stints. Because I had lived abroad and changed units a few times, I truly saw it in action. The people I served with were totally different from each other: street cleaners, teachers, bankers, professors, rich, poor and all in between. Miluim services were often very intense, and there was no difference between rich and poor or professor and street cleaner. It really felt like a hot melting-pot.

June 1982 also saw Britain and Argentina's war over the Falklands Islands. I was surprised that people in Britain who objected to the Lebanon war were in favour of the Falklands War. I don't believe Britain experienced the soul-searching about that war like Israel did over the Lebanon war. And there were no rockets fired from the Falklands into Britain.

in the borderlands

WORKING IN LONDON

I returned to England on 26 February 1984, the exact day Ya'akov Levinson committed suicide. It was important to me to work in a job connected to Israel, and I became head of the finance department of a large company with ties to it. During the period before moving again to England, I studied at the Tel Aviv branch of the Technion systems analysis, paid for by the bank.

It is instructive to contrast what happened in Israel to what happened in the rest of the world during the financial crash of 2008. The crash was a new experience for me, and we worried that some banks where the company had large deposits might go under. At the same time, many Israeli banks were not exposed at all and others very little: this is because, as a result of the local banking crisis of 1983, they were under strict supervision of the Bank of Israel. Although much smaller than the big international banks, the Israeli banks turned out to be safest. I really had many sleepless nights until things settled back to relative normality.

I have not personally witnessed a terrorist attack in Israel, but in July 2007 four suicide bombers blew themselves up on London transport, one just outside of our office in Tavistock Square. We heard the explosion, and the whole building shook. I was on the ninth floor and opened a window to see what had happened. The air had a strong smell of explosives; the roof of a bus was torn off, and you could see bodies and people walking in a haze. We were not allowed to go out. Later that day a person from Israel whom I vaguely knew contacted me, saying she now worked for one of Israel's TV channels and knew that our office was near where an explosion took place and the channel wanted to interview me. I described what I'd seen; a few people told me that they heard my report and, while I was speaking, my name was written over the screen, saying I was an Israeli working in London. The next day the channel contacted me again, asking me about the Israeli community in London. These TV interviews are my only claim to fame.

VISITING ISRAEL

My mother always had a list of items for me to repair during my weeklong visits; I also took her to shop and to visit her cousins in Ramat Gan and Tel Aviv. She loved to buy but was restricted by lack of money, so I would pay; she was like a child in a toy store, excitedly touching everything but not buying much. She also visited us in London; it was heartbreaking for me that I and her only grandchildren, whom she naturally adored, were so far from her. Emma's sister Celia, Julio and their four children were to some extent a replacement family; those children saw her as a grandmother, often visiting her and she them. In 1985, they moved from Ramat Gan to a new settlement in the West Bank called Ginot Shomron; it was both a political statement and a move for better quality of life, as now they had their own garden and village community. My mother was not happy: it made visiting them difficult, especially in the early days when the road to Ginot Shomron was through hostile Kalkiliya and other Arab enclaves. Only since 2018 does the journey no longer go through Arab villages, the last part of the bypass now completed. To avoid misunderstanding: Palestinians also use the bypass and most of the cars on that road have Palestinian number plates. I've also used buses to get to Ginot Shomron, on which the passengers are both Jews and Arabs. I made such a journey one Sunday, and the bus had many soldiers sitting near many Arabs; it seemed idyllic. Everyone put their bags in the hold under the seats and, if a terrorist were to have put a bag with a bomb, there would have been casualties among Jews and Arabs alike. Celia and Julio give their key to Abbas, a Palestinian living in a village not far away, when he works in their home.

I phoned my mother at least once a week on Sundays. She stayed young in spirit and attitude, and I try to copy her and not give in to age. People in Shafir helped her, but it was not ideal. For example, during the first Gulf War in 1991, when Saddam Hussein fired missiles into Israel and it was feared that they might carry chemical weapons, people in the moshav invited her to stay in their safe room; she did go a few times, but it was too much for her and she returned home where there was no safe room. Apparently Israeli pilots were ready to take off to fly to Iraq; at the time, everyone thought it was the wisdom of the then Israeli right-wing Prime Minister, Yitzhak Shamir, not to respond to Saddam, but we know now it was the Americans, who withheld the IFF or Identify Foe or Friend information, and Israeli pilots therefore could not fly to the war zone.

Sometimes I wonder what would have happened to me had I become a pilot. Most likely I would have given my parents a few heart attacks. But I always followed the air force with interest. Some of Israel's operations were more daring than in the movies, including the Entebbe rescue of Air France hostages in 1976, the bombing of Iraqi nuclear facilities in 1981 and of Syrian nuclear facilities in September 2007. In 2014, the area where Syrian nuclear facilities were held fell into the hands of ISIS; one may imagine what could have happened had they got hold of dangerous materials. Another operation was the rescue of Ethiopian Jews in 1991; a son of friends was one of the pilots on this mission. I think it was Colin Powell who commented that it was the first time in history that black people were brought to a country not for slavery but for freedom.

I mentioned that there was another terrorist incident in Shafir in addition to the one in 1956. In August 1988 Rachel Weisz, a Holocaust survivor in her seventies, was murdered by an Arab. The murder brought a journalist and photographer from the *Yediot Acharonot* newspaper to Shafir to capture its essence in an article. My mother is in one of the photos and her name is mentioned. When I visited her a few months later, I heard on the radio that the killer had been caught and the motive for murder was something like an initiation required for him to join a terrorist group in Gaza. This incident made me more worried about my mother living on her own in Shafir, but she was reluctant to move. The history of Israel has too many incidents of death, but to give them the right and sad perspective ninety-nine or so percent in the Middle East are of Muslims killing Muslims.

There were the Arab Intifadas, or uprisings, in 1987 and 2000, that left many dead, Israeli and Arab. This did not affect our trips, but I recall being more alert on the buses, at bus stops and in restaurants. One weekend, we stayed at Celia and Julio's place in Ginot Shomron and walked through the fields to another settlement called Maaleh Shomron to visit the family of a friend of our niece Tiri who had visited in London when Tiri was staying with us. This was totally stupid, and the friend's family did not allow us to return to Ginot Shomron on foot; they took us after Shabbat by car. On another visit, after staying again with Celia, I arranged that on the way back to Ramat Gan we would visit a friend in another settlement in the West Bank on a different road. The friend told me to take the first left after the army checkpoint, but when we did we found the road blocked by large concrete slabs. It was after Shabbat and very dark; we could see lights in the village behind the roadblock and turned around quickly, drove back to the checkpoint and were told we should turn left at the second road, not the first. The first turning was to a very hostile Arab village. I think my friend does not realise that hostile Arabs live so near to him. He is in a kind of denial.

A number of times I suggested to my mother that she leave Shafir and move to a retirement home, but she did not want to consider it. She also did not agree to my father-in-law's suggestion that she move to London to live in the same house as us, where a studio flat could be created for her. She said she could not face such an upheaval again after what she'd been through in her life. Eventually, as her friends in Shafir started to move to live near their children or some to die, she began to think that she might reconsider. Money was a factor, so I made a will with provision to support her if I predeceased her. A couple of times she agreed to move, and I made arrangements and bought tickets to fly to Israel to help, but then at the last minute she could not face it and cancelled it all. At last when her childhood friend Aranka, my father's cousin, decided to move to a retirement village in Ramat Efal near Ramat Gan, my mother agreed to do the same. I'd kept paying my membership of the trade union even though I lived in London so that my mother would be entitled to join this village, which belonged to it. We sold her home in the moshav to Avraham Levinger, whom we trusted; forty-one years of hard work yielded only one hundred thousand dollars. Avraham agreed to a condition that, if my mother were to change her mind during the first 24 months after the sale, it would be cancelled. At that time, real estate sales in Israel were transacted in US dollars because of inflation. My mother moved into Ramat Efal and realised what a mistake it was not to have moved earlier. At the end of the two years, Avraham sold the house to someone my mother did not trust and did not want to sell to, even though he offered 30% more. For me it was difficult, very difficult, that my connection to the place where I'd grown up was gone. Sadly, my mother's friend Aranka died not long after her moving, but my mother made new friends and became popular. She even acquired a close and nice gentleman friend.

My mother did not live long in Ramat Efal. After two and half years she was admitted to the nearby Tel Hashomer hospital with a perforated ulcer. She spent seven weeks there and contracted a super bug. I came from London every alternate week, and friends and family visited her often. Her new friends from nearby Ramat Efal also visited and I got to know them. As with my father in Kaplan hospital twenty years earlier, the Tel Hashomer staff's attitude and dedication were amazing. While in Israel, I spent most of my time there helping them. One Friday evening, the deputy head of department decided they should have a scan of my mother's heart and asked me to assist throughout the procedure, which I did. But as with my father, she did not have enough energy in her to fight and she died on 6 December 1993. Emma and I were planning to fly back to Israel that day; somehow my friends knew instantly that she had died. Avraham Levinger went to the hospital and dealt with arrangements to bury her in the Shafir cemetery, despite the fact that she had left the moshav. Rafi, my friend, worked out two possible flights from London and came to meet us at the airport at five in the morning to see how he could help. Ariel was studying in Paris and came later that day; Julio collected him and brought him directly to the funeral. A bus was arranged from the moshav to the cemetery; I put a death notice in the Hungarian newspaper, *Uj Kelet*, and sat shiva in Ramat Gan; many friends came to visit. Ariel commented that I was totally different in Israel than in London. In London I rarely answered the phone or made calls, while in Israel I was constantly on the phone to friends. Some of the friends visiting came from settlements and had guns. Emma did not feel comfortable seeing guns.

I was devastated by my mother's death, but not as angry as I had been at my father's. I was twenty years older and saw her deterioration, and although my father also spent some six weeks in hospital, we had thought he was getting better, so his end seemed sudden. Without exception, every trip I make to Israel, I visit the cemetery in the moshav and watch the older generation of Shafir slowly moving into it. Unfortunately, my generation also has representation there, even younger people and some soldiers.

On my visits I rarely go to Jerusalem. I don't have family there and only a few friends, and my trips are short with a lot to fit in. In addition, Jerusalem holds a special place in the heart, and one wants to think of it as holy and pure, so I don't want to see dirty streets and ugly new buildings. As is written in the song 'Yerushalayim shel Zahav',

> For your name scorches the lips
> Like the kiss of a seraph
> If I forget thee, Jerusalem
> Which is all gold...

VISITING CZECHOSLOVAKIA

The biggest international event in my lifetime was the fall of communism in 1989. For all of my life until then the world had lived under threat of nuclear catastrophe, and it felt very real. The world was divided into two, the West, led by the USA, and the East led by the USSR, with some countries forming what was called the Non-Alliance group. At least once the world was on the brink of a nuclear war, in 1962 when the US discovered that the USSR had deployed missiles in Cuba, very close to American shores. All the world followed that unfolding crises; I listened attentively to the radio. In Israel news used to be on the hour every hour; there is always news of life and death in Israel. The rest of the world was probably watching on TV, which may have been more frightening.

In 1991 I suddenly felt a desire to visit Czechoslovakia. I phoned my mother and suggested I take her with me; her reaction was, 'Why do you want to visit Czechoslovakia? They might kill you.' I don't remember the exact exchange, but she surprised me with her determination not to go back to her birth country – obviously memory of horrible experiences was still too strong. I then tried my aunt, whose reaction was similar. Once I had insisted that I was going, my mother agreed to give me what information she could about places and family. Unfortunately, after the death of her uncle, she had stopped corresponding with his children, fearing it would be detrimental for them to communicate with anyone in Israel, given how anti-Israel the Communist regime in Czechoslovakia was. My aunt for her part said she could not remember a thing. I phoned all the Urban phone numbers in Piestany that I could get from an international directory, but none of them were relatives. We flew to Prague and met up with Daniel Kummermann, a well-known dissident during Communist rule who later became the Czech ambassador to Israel and whom we would meet with his wife many times. The trip was an eye-opener as to how bad life had been under Communism. The old city of

Prague is very beautiful; from a Jewish perspective, incredible. As the Nazis had wanted to turn Prague into a museum for an extinct Jewish race, they did not destroy the Jewish quarter. In addition, they collected Jewish items from all over the country and brought them to Prague. I mentioned earlier our visit to the Jewish cemetery, but we went of course to all the other parts of the Jewish quarter and the rest of old Prague.

We then hired a car and drove to Bratislava, where we met an old friend of my mother's, with whom we communicated in Hungarian. She came with us to Samorin, the small town where she and my mother had lived. She showed me where my mother's home used to be – the house had been demolished to make room for a large building – and also the derelict synagogue and cemetery. I had no family members in this cemetery, as those living in Samorin had perished in the Holocaust. I told the friend that I was driving to Surany, the small town my father had come from; quietly, she told me not to go there as it was a very antisemitic place. I asked: 'How will they know I am Jewish?' I found, in Surany, an old man who spoke Hungarian and asked him directions to the cemetery, which he was happy to give. I then said, 'I mean the Jewish cemetery'; he said 'Same place', stopped the conversation and turned his back on us. We drove to the cemetery but could not find a Jewish section; eventually we were directed to a house onto which the cemetery backed. Everything was damaged and neglected, few tombstones were upright, the house-owner kept his animals in the cemetery. It was a demoralising experience. Over the years, the people living nearby had extended their properties over the grounds and used tombstones as building material.

We left and drove to the town centre. I got out of the car and was taking photos to show to my aunt; perhaps it would help her remember. I than ran back to Emma, who had stayed in the car, to tell her that I'd found the synagogue, which was now a warehouse. The reason I knew it was the synagogue was a Hebrew sentence carved in the stone above the entrance: 'veasu li mikdash veshachanti betocham' – 'And let them make Me a sanctuary, that I may dwell among them' (Exodus 25: 8). All other Jewish signs had been removed. A man in his sixties then approached; after trying to communicate in Slovak, German (I know little of these two languages) and Russian, we managed to do so in Hungarian, even though he hated the large Hungarian minority in that part of Slovakia. He was the mayor and wanted to know what we were doing. When I said my name was Klein and my father's family had lived in Surany for more than two centuries, he asked 'Heinrich Klein?' I said, 'That was the name of my grandfather.' He said he knew the family and, as a teenager, on Shabbat would do what Jews were forbidden to and get various items in return for it. He took us to his office; I told him what had happened in the cemetery and the synagogue; he replied that there were no longer any Jews in Surany. Pre-WW2, he said, half the town was Jewish. He took us to the house of my father near the synagogue but asked us not to go in as, in his words, a mad gypsy squatter lived there. I think he was afraid I would try to claim it back, though I had no such intention. He showed us where the yeshiva used to be, now a car park, and where the rabbi, the shochet (my father's first wife's home) and the doctor lived. He also showed us where Jews had been gathered and deported by rail; the onlookers had cried, he said. I of course don't believe any non-Jew had cried. A few months later, on a trip to Israel, I showed my aunt a photo of the house in Surany that the mayor said had been ours. My aunt told me it had not changed at all; she cried when I told her I could not find any family tombstones. There was, she said, a family plot and, as we were Cohanim or priests, it was near the cemetery's entrance. I hadn't even found where the real entrance was. As a Cohen, I don't enter cemeteries, but on the trip to my ancestors' past, I did try find what was left. Some years later, Emma was watching the TV programme 'Who do you think you are?' with Stephen Fry; his mother's family, who were Jewish, came from Surany. He and the team working on the programme found some of his family tombstones and the last and only Jew in the town.

With these unexpected discoveries, we left Surany later than planned and arrived in Piestany in the dark. We'd booked into the Eden hotel in the main street, as my mother had said that the family home was on that street. Everything in those days in Czechoslovakia was cheap, and the hotel was so cheap that I asked to see the room. It was beautiful, as was a blue marble bathroom. After the fall of Communism, many street names had been changed back to pre-Communism ones, but we could not find the family house. At the hotel, I asked if anyone knew of my great uncle, Alexander Urban, but no one spoke Hungarian or English. When I was about to give up, I heard an old woman, the toilet attendant, mumbling to herself 'Shani'. I recalled that the family had called my great uncle Shani, not Alexander, and nearly jumped on her saying yes, yes, Shani, Shani! She spoke Hungarian, probably the only one among thirty plus thousand inhabitants of the town to do so. She said that Hannka, the daughter, worked at reception in the Thermia hotel, starting at seven in the morning.

Next morning at seven I went to the Thermia on an island in the middle of the river. I asked to speak to Hannka Urban and was told the second door on the left. I entered and asked in English for her; one person responded, 'What do you want?' I looked at her and was amazed; she looked like my mother twenty years before. Her English was not great, but it was our only common language. I gave my name and explained who I was; she asked again what I wanted; I tried again but she still did not get what I said. Then I hit on an idea; I told her my mother's cousin Tibi from Israel had visited her; only then did she twig who I was and said 'Feri, Feri.' Stupid me, I should have known that her father only saw me as a baby and knew me as Feri, not Chaim. She said she would get the day off and take me to her home to meet her mother. After recovering, I told her my wife was still sleeping and we would meet her after breakfast. When we entered her impressive, big and very old house, both Emma and I felt as if we had walked into a museum. On its walls were large portraits of my great-grandparents, of which my mother had small copies, and everything was like in the 1930s. Hannka then drove us with her mother to the old Jewish cemetery, which had a fence and a gate. She had the key and took us to the family plot. As described in the opening paragraph of this memoir, I now stood in front of the large tombstones of my great-grandparents and next to them my grandmother's grandfather's tombstone! I never imagined I would see anything like it. I regularly call Hannka and we visit her and have stayed in the ancestral home. There are only a handful of Jews now living in Piestany, and nothing is left of the two synagogues.

If you want to join the Urban family in celebrating the centenary of their textile shop, I have a spare invitation; the only problem is that the centenary celebrations took place in 1937! On one of our later trips we met Ladislaw, Hannka's older half-brother; he and his younger brother as children during WW2 hid for years in the woods around Piestany; eventually they were betrayed and handed to the Nazis. They were deported to Bergen Belsen, from which they were liberated ten months later. He dedicated the last years of his life to increasing awareness of the Holocaust in Slovakia by appearing on TV and speaking on local radio, against the wishes of his family who worried about anti-Semitism. Emma wrote an article about him for *The Times*.

We have visited Surany twice more but have no intention of going again as it is too upsetting. Ariel joined us on a roots trip, which was instrumental in helping him leave behind his experience at the very orthodox Hasmonean School. Emma wrote a moving article for the Catholic weekly *The Tablet* about our trip called 'Lost World', part of which was broadcast on BBC World Service. I will quote one sentence from it: 'Visiting the graveyards and villages of south Slovakia brought home to me for the first time the reality of the lost world I had merely grasped with my mind, while living among survivors in the state of Israel.'

with Ariel, great-aunt Alice & Hannka at Piestany

LIVING LONG-TERM OUTSIDE OF ISRAEL

I was never happy living outside of Israel. As a friend said, 'We can take you out of the kibbutz, but we can't take the kibbutz out of you.' How true. I still don't like to wear shoes; I prefer sandals or bare feet. Even after living so many years abroad, I feel totally Israeli.

We made a few trips to Europe for holidays and I also had trips from work; each time on returning to London, I had to go through long queues at passport check. This was a headache when returning with family and they went through quickly as holders of British passports and had to wait for me. I decided to give in to practicality and start the process of obtaining a British passport. Both Israel and Britain allow dual nationality, so I have now two passports. I could ask for Slovakian passport too, but apparently it would be complicated – my birth certificate got lost in the upheaval of emigrating to Israel and early years there. My Israeli, and as a result my British, passport contains errors, the first being place of birth; the passports say Samorin, which is wrong. I only discovered the correct place of my birth in 1991. Before that first trip to Czechoslovakia, I'd asked my mother where exactly in Samorin I was born, and she replied, 'You were not born in Samorin but in Bratislava'. When I asked why then my Israeli ID and passport said Samorin, she did not know the answer. I assume that, in the confusion and language problems when we arrived at Israel, my parents were asked the place of my birth but assumed they were being asked the name of the town we'd come from. Another issue is my name: I use Chaim, but when I was born, as I discovered only in 2015, I was given also a Slovak name, Frantisek, after my mother's father. When I was very young, close relatives called me Feri, as mentioned, which I'd thought was only a nickname.

Though I live in the UK, I don't follow local news to the extent that I do Israeli news. When possible, I had the weekend Israeli paper *Yediot Acharonot* delivered to our home on Fridays and, since the internet took over, I read several Israeli media outlets each day, starting with *Ynet*, *Haaretz* and *Makor Rishon*. When people ask why I live in the UK, I explain that Emma is strict about the eleventh commandment. For some reason most people know only ten commandments, so if you also don't know the eleventh, here it is: 'Thou shall live in Hampstead only.'

Festivals are a difficult time for me in England, as it is so different from in Israel. In England 99.9% of people continue normal life, while in Israel even non-religious people celebrate to some extent. Another difficult time is when I return from Israel after a visit, life in the two countries being so different. On a recent visit I met a friend in Tel Aviv in the evening on the corner of Dizengoff and Ben Gurion Streets; there were thousands of people outside chatting to family, friends or strangers – it is such an open society! I always was happy to host and help friends and family from Israel who visited London; it was the kind of contact I looked for and needed. Both our sons went to what was an Israeli Sunday school; they did not like going as they preferred to play, but they did usually. I was the treasurer of this school, which was partly supported by the Israeli ministry of Education.

THE ASSASSINATION OF RABIN

When I was in the army Yitzhak Rabin was the chief of staff. I saw him a couple of times but don't recall the circumstances. On one occasion Rabin, with other dignitaries, was directed to a podium and, when he sat down, everyone saw that his socks were coloured and there was a laugh as it is forbidden for soldiers to wear coloured socks. There was something reassuring about Rabin; perhaps the slow and hesitant way he spoke, perhaps something in his looks or his shy smile – I don't know. Obviously, the glory of victory in the Six Day War helped. Certainly his qualities and career made him qualified to be prime minister. On the evening of the 4 November 1995, when he was assassinated, we were out with friends. When we came back, our younger son, who was living with us, told Emma what had happened. Amos knew that I would be very distressed, so he told Emma to tell me. Not only was I upset, I was also very angry. Rabin was assassinated by Yigal Amir, a right-wing student from Bar Ilan University, where I had studied years before. Rabin was attending a rally in favour of the Oslo accords with the Palestinians. Throughout the Oslo peace process, he had been under attack from right-wing parties; he was even portrayed as Hitler, and some right-wing rabbis declared din Rodef, or the law of the pursuer, on him. This legitimised murdering Rabin in the eyes of Amir, who wanted to stop the peace process. A Rodef in traditional Jewish law is one who is 'pursuing' another to murder him or her. According to that law, such a person must be killed by any bystander after being warned to stop and refusing. I don't have a problem in referring to and learning from ancient and traditional Jewish law, but I would say that declaring din Rodef on Rabin was criminal in itself. Unfortunately Amir succeeded, and we can only speculate on what would have happened to the peace process if Rabin had lived a few more years. Most world leaders, including King Hussein of Jordan and President

Mubarak of Egypt, attended Rabin's funeral. Just before his assassination, he had led the singing of 'Shir LaShalom' or 'The Peace Song'. The song, which expresses great yearning for peace, was written in 1969 and first sung by, of all people, a military ensemble – this was only two years after the great victory of the Six Day War. I find the song very powerful, with great tempo and energy about to burst into the open; it is, for me, the second most important song after 'Yerushalayim Shel Zahav'. In Rabin's pocket, a blood-stained sheet of paper with the words of the song was found. The assassination is a shameful episode in Israel's history. Talking about my two favourite songs leads me to mention song number three, 'Mah Avarech' or 'What Shall I Bless Him'. It was written after the Six Day War in memory of a fallen soldier and lists the features and talents he was blessed with. Its powerful ending is 'God God God, if only you blessed him with life'. It was sung by Rivka Zohar, who had the most beautiful voice. Sadly she had a tragic life.

ISRAELI ECONOMY

The Israeli economy evolved through a number of stages. As already mentioned, in the early years it was heavily state-controlled with high taxation; this was necessary to build foundations for the future while at the same time feeding the population, absorbing millions of newcomers and defending the country from its neighbours. There was a joke about Pinchas Sapir, the legendary finance minister (1955–1972): he was walking with one of Israel's biggest industrialists, who picked a small coin up off the pavement. Sapir expressed surprise: 'Why do you bother with such a small coin'? 'It is what is left for me out of every Lira I earn, because of your taxes', was the reply. Donations by Jews from around the world, selling government bonds and German reparation money helped Israel. In the early years, textiles were considered the engine driving the economy; Ata was the most famous textile company, and when my parents purchased clothing, it was Ata-made only. Israeli factories sold worldwide, for example to Marks & Spencer, Sears, Walmart and Calvin Klein (unfortunately no relation of mine). Textiles' role in Israel was compared to the car industry in the US. But lower wages in other countries forced closure of most of the Israeli textile factories, resulting in many redundancies, including that of my mother's cousin Tibi. One result of the peace agreements with Egypt and Jordan was that Israeli textile companies relocated there. Israel tried to develop a car industry, but it was not a success; some locally assembled cars were the subject of jokes. If you owned a Contessa, you were able to get into and drive any other Contessa and other Contessa owners could drive yours. Another car was called Susita; its body was made of fiberglass, which is not strong, so you had to be careful not to park it near animals as they would eat the fiberglass, i.e. the car. Today the roads in Israel and its towns are one big traffic jam; instead of developing public transport, most transport investment was directed for years to building roads and bridges, which only shifts the traffic jams, it doesn't solve anything. Only in the last few years has Israel started to invest in public transport.

While leaders were looking for a new engine to drive the Israeli economy, the Six Day War happened and took the country out of the then recession. Thousands of Arabs from Gaza and the West Bank started working in the country, and the Israeli and Palestinian economies benefited from each other. But after the Yom Kippur war, the Israeli economy was mismanaged, and the country suffered low growth coupled with inflation of up to 450%. A good definition of inflation is when someone buys a property for say a million and later sells it for say two million but in real terms the transaction results in a loss. In 1985, a unity government was able to bring inflation under control; a stabilization programme and structural reforms similar to those in other world economies were introduced. The economy then gradually opened up, resulting in rapid growth in the 1990s. Polishing and trading in diamonds became a major sector, but it was not an engine to drive the economy. There were ups and downs, but the big catalyst for improvement was over one million new immigrants, mainly from countries of the former USSR. Also, there were major technological changes happening in the world, and the military was in the forefront of developing and implementing those changes in Israel, propelling growth. Israel leads in the use of the sun for energy; in 2019 it ranked second in the world in the use of solar power as a percentage of total energy use (8.7%). But this is not enough; it should do much more. When I was seventeen, we started to have hot water by installing cheap solar panels on the roof. Many of those coming back from the military into civilian life had knowledge and experience to enable them to become start-up entrepreneurs. The country transformed into a start-up nation with an unprecedented inflow of foreign investment. I followed, as part of my job, a number of start-ups through the stage of ideas to achievement of success or failure. Many Israeli start-ups were sold, making their founders multi-millionaires. Some claim there are two economies in Israel: the high-tech one and the ordinary old fashioned one. The Israeli Shekel is strong, partly because Israelis who benefit from the sale of start-ups change the dollars they receive into shekels, increasing demand for the currency and its value.

Today the gap between rich and poor in Israel, as in most of the world, is too big. The capitalist model has a lot of advantages; for initiative, freedom and prosperity, it beats the communist model. But the gap between rich and poor is out of control; it is bad full stop, but in a country like Israel, which is small and still under existential threat, it undermines togetherness and affinity between people, which is essential. The gap is also against Jewish law and tradition, so more checks and balances are required.

KFAR HAMACCABIAH

To my delight Ariel and Alix got married in Israel and nearly all the participants from abroad stayed in Kfar Hamaccabiah. I noticed that the hotel was planning to build an extension where it would be possible to buy flats in a scheme called 'second home in Israel' for people living abroad. The flats, ranging from studios to three-bedrooms, would be part of the hotel but the owners and their family and friends could stay there with two weeks' notice. I wanted to buy a one bedroom flat but thought the price was too high; Kfar Hamaccabiah refused to lower the price, and I did not buy. After the wedding, on each visit to Israel, I would check whether the hotel would negotiate the price, but they refused. Even after the building was completed they refused, so I told them that if someone who'd bought a flat wanted to sell, let me know. Not long after, I was contacted by the hotel, telling me that an Argentinian person had to sell his flat and, after some negotiation, Emma and I bought it. We absolutely love the flat, the hotel and the area;

it is near Tiri and her family and not too far from our other niece, Mali. Usually, Celia and Julio stay with us from Friday until the end of Shabbat; Celia and Tiri cook and we have great time. Celia and Julio no longer have a car, so Emma and I drive to Ginot Shomron to bring them and the food and to see our nephews: Boaz and his family also live in Ginot Shomron; Yoni lives even deeper in the West Bank, at Kedumim near Nablus. Some of our friends, both in Israel and London, are surprised and worried and ask if we are not afraid driving around in the West Bank but that's where some family and friends live, so we visit them.

On a flight back to London after the wedding of Ariel and Alix, a Charedi young man was seated next to me. As Emma was seated further away, I asked if he would mind swapping with her. The Charedi responded that God made him sit there and he would not move; I told him that God made me sit next to him in order for me to ask him to move away. This totally confused him; luckily, we managed to get the person sitting on my other side to swap with Emma. During the flight, I chatted with the Charedi; he was one of sixteen siblings and had five children, one born with severe disabilities, and he was coming to London to ask fellow Jews to help by giving him money. He said he had heard that in London there were rich people who could fill a swimming pool with money. He did not go to the army as he pretended that he was studying; in fact, he told me, he was earning money by writing by hand, on parchment, mezuzot, which are on doors of Jewish homes, and tefillin. He did not know what tax was, and he was primitive and unknowledgeable not only about secular studies but also about religious ones. When I found out that he only had fifteen pounds on him yet intended to travel from the airport to Stamford Hill, I checked how much cash I had and how much I needed to get home and gave him the difference. Not only was he surprised but I was surprised at myself, as I do not like to give cash to people for charity in order not to tempt them to cheat. He grabbed the money and kind of thanked me.

I recall two other Charedi encounters in my life. The first was when I joined the army. With us was a Charedi person, which was rare. Even in uniform, he looked different, with a long beard and peot, or side curls. He was a little older and totally useless – perhaps, when we were training with guns, even dangerous. He was picked on and mocked, and I felt sorry for him. He ended up working in an army kitchen as a cook and Kosher supervisor. The other Charedi was a rabbi in our building in Ramat Gan. He and his wife lived on the first floor, and each year they had one or two (twins) more children. They looked and were totally different from everyone in the area; the oldest girl had to look after the younger ones, and she and those close to her in age had no childhood. When I was on Vaad Habait, or the house committee, and went into their flat, I saw that the children were sleeping in a double-bed along the width not the length, like sardines.

CHANGES IN THE ZIONIST RELIGIOUS MOVEMENT

It was relatively straightforward in the early years of Israel to be a moderate religious person; I described this within our moshav when I was a child. Much changed over the years, and there are many different currents and subcurrents nowadays. From the time of the establishment of Israel, Hamizrachi and Hapoel Hamizrachi were partners of Mapai, the party that led all coalition governments in the early years. In 1956, Hamizrachi and Hapoel Hamizrachi merged and became Miflaga Datit Leumit (Mafdal) or the Religious National Party. After the Six Day War, Mafdal was still a moderate party but the younger members pushed it more and more to identify with the settlement movement. In all elections until 1981, the party received about ten percent of the vote. In 1977 the right-wing parties headed by Menachem Begin won the election for the first time, and Mafdal joined Begin's coalition government, moving more to the right. In the 1981 election, the vote for the party halved and never recovered. Between 1992 and 1996 it was in opposition; the prime minister was Labour's Yitzhak Rabin and, after his assassination, Shimon Peres, but the Mafdal remained in opposition. In 2003, in the wake of Ariel Sharon's disengagement from Gaza and parts of the north of the West Bank, Mafdal split and those that left it joined eventually 'Haichud Haleumi' or 'The National Union'. The National Union was a merger between Moledet (homeland), Tekuma (rising) and, for a while, Israel Beiteinu' (Israel our home). The word 'religious' disappeared from the title of the party, and it was now firmly at the very right of the political spectrum. The Mafdal was dissolved on 3 November 2008, and I felt a bit of a Zvita Balev, or pinch in my heart. If you are confused, it is because it is confusing. Changing names, mergers, splits are familiar in Israeli politics and the Zionist religious movement had more than its fair share. Adding to the mix was my teacher, Tova Ilan, who, as mentioned, was a founder in 1988 of Meimad, the moderate political religious movement. I know many politically moderate religious people, but the media likes to ignore them. Meimad did not last for long and only had two members in the Knesset at its height. In 2019, after more splits and mergers, a non-religious (but of course right-wing) woman, Ayelet Shaked, became head of the religious party.

Many in the Zionist religious movement find today's HaRabanut HaRashit, the body heading the rabanut, too strict, corrupt, political and out of touch with contemporary life. The Charedi community, now controlling the rabanut, wants to benefit from the state of Israel but not to contribute, which is not sustainable in the long run. The rabanut is recognised and financed by the state, but this is not reciprocated. During our long exile, religion ensured the survival of Judaism, but modernity has changed this, and Zionism is a secular not a religious movement; one can even be a Zionist and a non-Jew. Zionist religious movements more than fully participate in every aspect of life in Israel; nowadays they are in the forefront of the Army elite combat units, replacing the kibbutzim and moshavim. Similarly, they help more than any other groups in socially deprived parts of the country. They are going through big changes: today a religious homosexual or lesbian will not be ostracised; women study gemmarah and say kaddish, and there are partnership minyanim where women actively participate in the services and are committed to the Halacha, or religious law. In the diaspora, non-religious Jews tolerate religion more than Israeli non-religious people, partly because Israelis feel there is religious coercion in their country; also, religion in the diaspora still has a role in preserving Judaism and protecting against assimilation. The youth movement 'Bnei Akiva' was associated with the Mizrachi party, and it was the only youth movement where I lived when I was growing up. Unlike today, in all Bnei Akiva activities – and there were many – there was no segregation between boys and girls.

For a few years I read in the newspapers about the first religious pilot girl in the air force. Her name and where she was living were not given, only that she was from a settlement in the south. Tragically she died in a snow avalanche on holiday in Nepal. It did not surprise me that she was from Massuot; I did not know her family. Her commander said she was implacably religious, allocating time for prayer three times a day, but otherwise much like every other pilot. There is a documentary film about her life and she is buried in the same cemetery as my parents. It took some fifty years for Israel to train girls as fighter pilots and another fifteen for one of these girls to be a religious one.

COIN AND BANK NOTE COLLECTIONS

While working in Bank Hapoalim, I was once in a branch when someone walked in with an envelope of old bank notes, out of circulation and no longer legal tender. When I was young, I had known that these notes existed but had never seen any, as they were of high value. The family of the person with the notes had found them in a drawer when a grandfather died. The notes were so old that the branch could not help, and the person was told to go to Tel Aviv to the Bank of Israel at 1 Rothschild Boulevard. I overheard the clerk telling the man that he would only get face value for the notes, which would just about cover a bus ride to Tel Aviv and back. I offered the man a little more and bought them off him. I was always drawn to old things attached to our history; also, I could not resist having something I could not have had in the past. I suppose I also wanted things that most families pass down the generations but that the Holocaust and moving between countries had reduced in our case to very few items. I had two or three similar occasions in branches, enabling me to buy old bank notes and coins; this is how I started a collection.

I have examples of all notes that were legal tender in Israel since its creation. The first ones in 1948 were issued by Bank Anglo Palestine; later the bank changed its name to Bank Leumi LeIsrael or National Bank of Israel, thus the notes were issued by Bank Leumi. I have a few also from the time of the British Mandate, which were legal tender for the first four months after the establishment of Israel. From 1952, notes were issued by the state; they were simple and small as befitted a regime of rationing. It was only in 1955 when a central bank, The Bank of Israel, was formed, that they were issued by that bank, as has been the case ever since. Because of inflation the Lira changed to Shekel (23/2/1980) which changed to New Shekel (31/12/1985). In time, security features on the notes became sophisticated to prevent forgery. I also collect the coins of Israel, but I don't have all the gold and memorial ones issued, as there are too many and it would have cost too much and I would have had a problem of where to keep them. I think the state-owned company issuing them overdid the number, which makes them not a good investment. I have about sixty ancient coins, including from the time of the Maccabees, the first revolt against Rome in 70 AD and the second in 134 to 137 AD. The oldest coin I have is Alexander the Great from 336 to 323 BCE. I have one of Antiochus vii 138 BCE; the Chanukah Antiochus is number iv. From collecting Israeli notes only, I expanded to collecting others. The oldest bank note I have is dated 1717 and from Sweden.

BOOKS AND HAGGADOT

As a teenager, I asked my father to buy the five books of the Torah with as many commentaries as possible (called Rav

Pninim or many pearls) and the Even Shushan Hebrew Dictionary (five volumes). My father bought them, paying by instalment over two years. Once I had money, I ended up with thousands of books. I bought bibles, prayer books, Haggadot, books about the Hebrew language, books about Israel and the Holy Land. I had about thirty books about early travel there, mainly in the 19th century, and read them all. One thing I noticed was that most of these books were written by visitors, not locals, and there were 'black holes' in the history. From the beginning to the present, this small track of real estate, sole place on Earth to be called 'Holy Land', has been fought over again and again. For Judaism it is the only Holy Land, but it is also central to Christianity and Islam. Many old maps show Jerusalem at the heart of the world; I have some. The Holy Land is the connecting bridge between Asia and Africa and, by extension, between Europe and Africa. Interestingly, it was never an empire like its neighbours Egypt, Babylon, Persia, Greece or Turkey, but it was always important religiously and culturally.

This 'centre of the world' was for hundreds of years neglected, vandalised, unsafe, with large parts uninhabited and no rule of law. The picture from accounts of 19th century pilgrims about the lifestyle of inhabitants, agriculture and farming systems, access to water for domestic and farm use, transport methods and 'roads', is that little had changed since Biblical times. Famous cities like Jerusalem, Jaffa and others were secured by walls and gates; conditions were anarchic, even desperate. Mark Twain wrote of his visit in 1867: 'Palestine sits in sackcloth and ashes... desolate and unlovely... hardly a tree or a shrub anywhere... We never saw a human being on the whole route.' W. H. Bartlett wrote in *Walks About the City and Environs of Jerusalem* (1842): 'Beautiful but lifeless expanse...

the city looked wholly lifeless and forsaken.' I could go on. By the way, Jews living in the Holy Land, mainly Jerusalem, Tsfat, Tveria, Hebron, Gaza and Jaffa were, according to these pilgrims, like the rest of the inhabitants: dirty, lazy and generally off-putting.

The ultimately unsuccessful attempt by Napoleon to conquer the Holy Land in 1799 is the earliest significant event in the modern history of the place. We can speculate on what prompted him to embark on this ill-fated war, a continuation of his successful occupation of Egypt, which had triggered little response from the Turks. Napoleon's expedition put the Holy Land back into the international arena and helped to disintegrate the Ottoman Empire. The 19th century heralded big changes in many parts of the world, including the Middle East. Use of steam made transportation, both by land and sea, more accessible and dramatically increased the number of pilgrims; education and academia in Europe and America expanded and with it greater scholarly interest in the Holy Land. Nationalism took hold and larger numbers of Jews escaping persecution in Europe made their home in the Middle East. Unlike Jews already living there, newcomers wanted to work and not live on World Jewry donations. They cleared swamps, created new settlements and cultivated the land; most were not religious. As the Ottoman Empire weakened, the then world powers started to take more interest in the region. Consuls were appointed, the British in 1838 followed by German, French, American and others; by 1865 there were eleven in total. The fact that Christianity and Judaism had a strong presence in the Holy Land gave them an opening to play a more substantial role in its affairs as compared to other places in the world.

One 19th century episode too little known is the conquest of the Holy Land in 1831 (until 1840) by the Egyptian army of Mehmet Ali. This brutal and cruel son of an Albanian fisherman was a moderniser and, with the help of his stepson, Ibrahim Pasha, reorganized the bureaucracy and tax systems of the region, restored law and order and developed commerce and agriculture. Probably in an attempt to bring European powers to his side vs. the Turks, he liberalised the rights and status of Christians and Jews, allowing them to purchase homes and repair their places of worship. For the first time in hundreds of years the Holy Land was unified into one political-administrative unit.

There is a phenomenon called Holy Madness. The late Mira Hamermesh, whom we knew, made a TV programme about it, which Emma reviewed for *The Times*. Visitors to Jerusalem are sometimes carried away by the spirituality of the place – everywhere one sees clergymen, Jewish, Muslim and Christian of many sects, all wearing special gowns. The holy places and strange land add to the mix, and some start to believe they are the reincarnation of Jesus, Abraham, Moses or other Biblical figures to an extent that they need medical attention. I have no knowledge of any 19th century pilgrim affected by such madness, but many certainly felt as if they were transported back to Biblical times.

The biggest group of books I have are the Hagadot. I have about three hundred, the majority collected just because I liked them and they were not expensive. I do have some that would cost a few hundred pounds but nothing fancy. I started collecting them when a great aunt of Emma's died and her many old Jewish/prayer books were given to a synagogue. I asked for the Hagadot that had been in Emma's family since 1880, when her great uncle bought them. They include Hagadot published in Jerusalem in 1904 and 1905 and later, others published in Livorno, Italy in 1880 and some published in Baghdad, also in 1880. The book I'm most proud of was printed in Denmark in 1776; it is volume B of the full year-round prayers, daily and the festivals. I tried to find volume A but did not succeed.

MEDIA AND ISRAEL

Living abroad while closely following what happens in Israel makes me, I think, more sensitive than many to international media coverage. Does coverage of the Arab-Israeli conflict affect Israeli policy? Of course, but in a contradictory and complex way. We live in an era of worldwide round the clock instant news and our interest is not limited to news that might affect us but, with the help of social media, anything that is happening anywhere pops up live in our palm wherever we are and while it is unfolding. Any story, especially with a human aspect, may capture our attention even if superficially; a goods train accident near our home with no casualties may, if reported, not attract us but a commuter train accident elsewhere in the world with casualties may be a major news item watched by millions. Vivid scenes of the horrors of war, with many innocents suffering, touch most of us; as anti-war demonstrations show, huge numbers believe war is an unnecessary evil.

For decades, the Middle East has been a centre of attention, as a seemingly everlasting conflict with repeated flare-ups has not been resolved. Given the religious and historic significance of the Holy Land, it is unrealistic for it to be treated, as Israelis demand, like any other of the many territorial conflicts around the world; too many people, even those who do not appear to have a personal connection to the region or its issues, are emotive about this conflict. Israelis see themselves, given the enormous territorial and population differences, as David against Goliath, but many in the rest of the world see it the other way round. The feeling in Israel of being under siege is compounded by what Israelis see as biased reporting; they follow the media closely and describe it as a 'war'.

In the military sphere, the most dramatic change brought about, primarily by negative reporting, is in strategy. From small mobile units which can move quickly into enemy territory, Israel is now investing in defensive hardware. The most spectacular is the Iron Dome, a mobile, all-weather missile defence system. It has intercepted about 90% of rockets that might have landed in populated areas, calculating within seconds whether a just-fired rocket will hit such an area or not and ignoring rockets that won't. Other defensive tools include physical obstacles created in the hills of the Galilee on the northern border with Hezbollah and an underground/overground concrete wall, mainly against tunnels, along the border with Gaza. Added to these defences is the part-barrier/part-wall in the West Bank and Jerusalem. The view of Israelis is that they are creating a 'villa in the jungle', pointing to years of full-blooded mayhem unconnected to Israel raging in the Arab world. Again, many in the outside world see it differently.

With so much 'collateral damage' – i.e. effect of war on innocents – at the centre of media attention, Israelis claim that Hamas, which controls Gaza, seeks deliberately to increase civilian casualties by positioning rocket launchers and other weapons in schools and heavily populated areas. But there are additional reasons why there is an imbalance in civilian casualties: Israel has invested in shelters and, for years, all new buildings or even those undergoing renovation, have to include 'safe rooms'. There is nothing like this on the Palestinian side. Also, Israel possesses much more powerful weapons and the population density in Gaza is much greater. Israel investigates all civilian casualties, and the makeup of its military resembles the population at large, so any unit will include soldiers who object to the occupation and will report any misdeed. There are also quite a few organisations which seek to expose wrongdoing, and some soldiers complain that a large number of claimed incidents are the result of deliberate lies or 'the fog of war' since a field soldier can't see the full picture. Israelis feel that they are obliged to defend themselves with one hand tied behind their back. In the last few Gaza conflicts, Israel dropped leaflets, sent messages to mobile phones and introduced a 'knock on the roof' policy to give advance warning of impending bombing, firing a specially developed very small rocket at the target. However, these measures and the continual development of more precise weapons will not eliminate all 'collateral damage'.

Of particular concern to Israelis is the BDS (Boycott, Divestment & Sanctions) movement. While admitting that many BDS supporters mean well, Israel points out that the movement does not advocate a peaceful solution but elimination of Israel. This is used by many Israelis to advocate an 'ignore the world' policy, as no matter what Israel may do the world will be against Israel. They claim that Israel is singled out and compare it to the pre-WW2 era when Jews were singled out, leading to mass killing. This gives a tailwind to those who push for settlement expansion, which complicates a future solution even more. The so-called UN Human Rights Commission – 'so-called' because in many of the states of members of the commission, human rights hardly exist – came up in 2020 with a blacklist of companies operating in areas beyond the old green line. AirBNB, Booking.com and Trip Advisor, for example, operate in other parts of the world the UN describes as occupied territories, but only in Palestinian areas are their operations blacklisted. To many living in the area, it seems that the UN Commission and the BDS don't care about the Palestinians but just want to damage Israel, even if it damages Palestinians too.

To illustrate how anti-Israel people can be, many cite the latest translation of the Bible into Danish, published in 2020, by the Danish Bible Society. It omits references to Israel, replacing them with 'Jews' or 'us' or 'everyone'. The Danish Bible Society explained that they wanted to avoid confusion between the land of Israel and the state of Israel, but they did not change, for example, ancient Egypt.

REUNION

Our school class had a reunion in 2003, and I would have loved to have had more. As I live abroad, I meet only a few friends regularly and have no contact with most others. I do hear via those with whom I'm in contact what is happening to many classmates and members of the moshav. In the early years, after moving to the UK, I encountered a few incidents when people said things that indicated displeasure that I was not living in Israel. Yitzhak Rabin described those emigrating from Israel (yordim or going down) as nefolet nemushot, or the mediocre weak. In contrast, at school I always felt I was in the centre of activities and popularity. On reflection, I think that I and some of my closest friends were not, when growing up, inclusive enough of others, who were perhaps not such good pupils or sporty.

SHAFIR IS SEVENTY

I flew to Israel to attend a gathering of the children of the founders of Shafir, scheduled to take place in March 2019

but cancelled because of rockets fired from Gaza; nevertheless I did go to Shafir and met a few old friends. In September of that year, Shafir commemorated the seventieth anniversary of establishment of the moshav, and I flew again to Israel, my fourth visit in less than a year. The gathering was fantastic; I met people I had not seen in six decades and only recognised when they said their name, as we were children when they left the moshav. There were others I had not seen for fifty, forty, thirty or twenty-five years. We had all changed, some more, some less; I recognised most. Three or four people commented on how popular and special my mother had been. The moshav has changed so much: there are roads, pavements, well-maintained gardens and lots of trees. Over the years the number of families with cows had gone down, as people looked for easier options like growing flowers, peanuts, sweet corn or squash. Today there are only four families with cows, and they produce vastly more milk than the hundred did in the early years. There are strict environmental restrictions. With growing demand all over the country from children to live in the moshavim and kibbutzim where they grew up, land used for agricultural purposes had to make room for houses. This happened in Shafir. The standard of buildings and infrastructure in the Harchava, or extension, was high and resulted in a serious upgrade of infrastructure everywhere in the moshav. I already wrote about a family with five children who all made their home in Shafir. I met some grandchildren of founders who had moved to towns and had successful careers but wanted to move back to Shafir while continuing to work in towns, even Tel Aviv. Today there are about half a million Israelis living in moshavim, and there is pressure to allow more and more residential building on agriculture land to ease housing shortages. If the trend continues, it may help with those shortages but it may create some food shortages. One can't view agriculture only from an economical perspective; it is part of national security since a country can't be dependent on others for food.

The moshav created a website to remember its founders and early years. It is a moving project, started by volunteers. As none of the founders' generation is alive, their children, with input from present younger members of the moshav, populate the site. The founders are all listed: photos, documents and family details are posted; memories of our early life in the moshav, recalled by individuals, are available and fascinating to read. The Holocaust hovers in the background of each. One story, by a child of a founder who left Shafir early – I don't remember the family – caught my eye. The mother was from Samorin, same as my mother, and her experiences in the Holocaust were similar. Apparently, there were 350 Jews in Samorin, only sixteen of whom survived. I tried to get in touch with the family but did not succeed; I wanted to know how they got their information and what else might be learned. I'd been searching for some time for documents about my parents during WW2 – it has now more possible as more records are appearing online – and shortly after finishing this memoir, I discovered that on 16 April 1944 a ghetto was established around the synagogue in Samorin, from where all Jews were transferred to Auschwitz. I then found a registration document, dated 8.9.1944, of my mother into Dachau. I had not known she was in Dachau! The document gives a detailed physical description of her and general information and states that she was arrested on 8.6.1944, the reason given as 'J' i.e. 'Jewish'. The document says that she was transferred from Auschwitz and is signed by my mother – I recognise the signature. She reduced her age by eleven years, not changing the day or month, probably to improve her chance of staying alive. Knowing that she gave her year of birth as 1925 enabled me to find another document, from which it seems that she arrived to Dachau with nothing. From a document in Hungarian signed by her and dated 26.7.1945 it seems that, after liberation, she was sent to Budapest. I also found a copy of an announcement from 5 December 1941 that the family business in Piestany has been taken over.

Information about my father came from his claim for reparations. He was arrested in March 1944, not in Surany but in nearby Nove Zamky (was he hiding?) and 'supplied' to the Hungarian forced labour battalion WEP 106. In December '44 he was sent to Bucau in Romania, probably with a Hungarian battalion. It seems that he arrived in Mauthausen only in March '45 and in April was transferred to a sub-camp called Gunskirchen, from which he was liberated by the US army on 5 May. In public records I found that the construction of Gunskirchen had started in December '44 and in April '45 thousands of prisoners – my father must have been one – were evacuated on death marches, on foot, from Mauthausen and flooded Gunskirchen, which had become very overcrowded. Diseases such as typhus and dysentery spread through the starving and weakened population. A US soldier's eyewitness account states that the camp was 'littered with corpses… Almost every inmate was insane with hunger… about 1500 died after liberation from what they endured before.' After liberation my father, like my mother, was transferred to Budapest, arriving on 26/6/1945. One wants to know what happened and, when one finds out, it is overwhelming and paralysing. Separately, I found a document in Slovak from the municipality of Surany, dated 23 August 1945 confirming that my father was entitled to live in Surany and his address was Masarik Street No 17.

At the beginning of this memoir I wrote that we lived in a tent. After reading the stories of others, I realised something I remembered was correct even if it seemed unbelievable. We were two families in that tent! I recall even that I was told who the family living with us was, but did not write this because I thought it was impossible. The other family were Latzi and Lili Friedman, whom I already mentioned.

BEFORE ENDING

The idea to write this memoir came up a few years ago when I was driving Ariel and his family to Heathrow to fly to Israel. Alix was asking questions about the past and Ariel kept saying I had to write it all down. I have been asked if writing this memoir was therapeutic. I don't think so: it kept me awake at night many times, as more and more memories came back. I was also asked once if I am driven. I always thought of myself as not driven. I just wanted to do well enough so that I would not be embarrassed, and to earn enough so as not to be under stress. I am a strong believer in moderation; this is applicable to everything. In my early fifties, a friend of mine about my age, suddenly left his good and secure job for no apparent reason. When another friend, also in his fifties, said 'midlife crisis', I said 'but we are also in our 'midlife''; my friend replied that he and I were too 'square'. I was told once by someone that I could have not achieved what I achieved without being driven. Perhaps I should leave it to others to decide whether I'm driven or not.

PEACE?

I leave to the end the most important issue facing Israel since before its establishment, but there is little I can say about peace in the Middle East. There has been some progress but sadly also regression. I have no doubt that the majority of both Israelis and Arabs want to live in peace, but extremism and lack of leadership does not make it happen. One can only hope that somehow there will be peace, and sooner rather than later.

***

Lightning Source UK Ltd.
Milton Keynes UK
UKHW020656271221
396186UK00007B/217

9 780936 315492